toward a more

SIMPLE, PLAIN

and

RATIONAL ENGLISH

toward a more
SIMPLE, PLAIN
and
RATIONAL ENGLISH

SWARNA

PARTRIDGE
A Penguin Company

Partridge books may be ordered through booksellers or by contacting:

Partridge India
Penguin Books India Pvt.Ltd
11, Community Centre, Panchsheel Park, New Delhi 110017
India
www.partridgepublishing.com
Phone: 000.800.10062.62

CONTENTS

introduction. xi

1. word classes 1

2. personal pronouns 9

3. nouns and their plural forms 13

4. adjectives 18

5. Verbs 25

6. irregular verbs. 34

7. causative verbs 41

8. modal auxiliaries. 45

9. tenses 50

10. prepositions 59

11. adverbs. 67

12. question words and question phrases 70

13. discourse markers 72

14. sentence patterns 82

15. passive voice. 90

16. types of clause 95

17. reported speech 104

18. dynamics of communication 119

19. language and culture 128

20. spelling and pronunciation. 137

21. varieties of english 141

22. Story telling 145

        last word. 167

['truth is no different than a mere blind belief unless truth is put in the right perspective with all the circumstances and reasons adduced to prove it so.' Dharmavyadha in mahabharat]

a critique of the structure of the english language, in particular, and language, in general.

also a critique of the religious notions, irrational beliefs and ridiculous practices of the people who allow themselves to be exploited by fraudsters, claiming superhuman powers with the tools of magicians and declaring themselves to be incarnations of god.

S v subbarao, b a (hons)

PREFACE

This book can be used as any other grammar book. Simple rules are set down for generating and transforming structures and graduated exercises are provided at end of each chapter to test students' competence in the understanding and the use of well-formed structures.

What is grammar? What works is science; it is said simply yet elegantly. What works in performing speech acts is grammar. It requires a certain competence to perform speech acts. The native speaker acquires this competence through observation and imitation right through infancy. But others have to acquire the competence through a totally conscious effort, for there are no models who to observe and imitate. The grammar of a language equips you with the competence that not only enables you to communicate clearly without ambiguity but also gives you the necessary confidence to do so in real life situations. It is sincerely hoped that this book will help you gain the competence and the confidence. It also answers such questions as why certain structures are considered well-formed and certain other structures, not so well-formed.

First and foremost, we have to see whether correct and appropriate structures are used. Second, we should check whether the ordering of the structures in the sentence makes the communication clear and unambiguous. For example, we will consider the expression, well established in the American usage and fairly common in other varieties also, "We kindly request you to take your seats." (Garner's Modern American usage) The problem with this expression is not as simple as the misplacing of the word 'kindly'. The problem is whether we should split the infinitive, because that is the only place for 'kindly' to make the expression unambiguous thus: "We request you to kindly take your seats." This results in splitting the infinitive, which proves the point that there is nothing wrong in splitting an infinitive in order to make an expression clear and unambiguous.

There are also a number of other totally useless conventions not only in English but in almost all other modern languages. Therefore I address the following question to the experienced practitioners of English. Should we not dispense with these conventions to make English, the only language, at present, with a truly global reach, simple and easy to learn and use?

INTRODUCTION

"truth is no different than a mere blind belief unless truth is put in the right perspective with all the circumstances and reasons adduced to prove it so." Dharmavyadha in mahabharat

origin of speech
is speech species-specific?

even the ancients knew that speech was a special faculty of humankind. the language is species—specific, according to chomsky, and the ability of its acquisition is genetically transmitted from human beings to their progeny. as the universal grammar is wired into a child's brain before it is born, it can acquire the language of the native speakers among whom it is brought up. is speech acquisition a special faculty which human beings alone possess? perhaps, there were, on this planet, some species, now extinct, which had the faculty of speech. it is also in the realm of possibility that there are or were, on some other planet of some other star quite like our sun, in this or in some other universe, some organisms which transmit and receive information the way we do, that is, through speech. then, what are the special conditions or circumstances, which necessitate, facilitate and bring about the acquisition and the use of speech as we know it?

first, the organisms, in order to adopt and cultivate speech, have to be surrounded by air through which alone the vibrations, stimulating hearing, travel with little hindrance.

second, the organisms should be gregarious. a social life is both necessary and desirable for the humans, as their young ones are helpless at birth and for quite some time thereafter. besides, they themselves live in a hostile world and mostly lead a precarious existence, sharing the same space and habitat with other animals vastly superior to them in physical strength and agility.

third, they should adopt an upright posture and mobility, thus, freeing their forearms to make gestures, handle tools and create symbols. it appears that the earliest attempts at communication were pictographic or ideographic symbols. chinese script is the same, though the speech that originally evolved from the common written symbols differs from region to region. writing followed speech is too facile a generalization to be applied universally. the reason why we have not been able to decipher the script of mohanjadaro and harappa lies in our misconception that speech always preceded writing.

like evolution of species, civilizations have probably taken different paths. it is possible that some civilizations developed some sort of elaborate writing systems for communication and they perished, for reasons unknown to us, before they evolved oral communications based on those systems or independent of them.

the upright posture alone can allow the species to have a clear understanding of the message communicated through facial expressions, gestures and visual symbols which pre-existed and eventually prompted utterance of sounds. the sounds which accompanied, reinforced and complemented the message contained in the gestures, symbols and facial expressions became customized and structured into speech to which the facial expressions etc. are now complementary.

fourth, the species should have the organs in the mouth, capable of producing sufficient number of distinct sounds.

fifth, and above all, a species, to acquire, retain and develop speech, should possess a brain large enough to store, retain, process and retrieve information when needed. It is also true that the language accelerates the growth and development of brain, particularly its active folder, a critical amount of which is required for the acquisition and practice of speech. The brain—body ratio of the humans is the highest among all of the mammals.

sixth, the young ones of the species, in order to acquire speech, should have a slow enough growth in order to absorb the software, that is, the speech of the community in which it lives. the species should also have a long enough life-span and considerable free time for observation and contemplation. the humans have one of the longest life-spans among mammals and the human young ones take quite a long time to attain maturity and their adult members enjoy long spells of free time, gained through adoption of tools and division of work among the members of the family and the community at large.

origin of speech
is chomsky's theory of universal grammar scientific?

the pattern of sounds vocalized in a particular situation, out of fear, surprise, affection, joy sorrw or simple recognition of a familiar object, as an instinctive response of an individual's nervous system to a stimulus external or internal becomes a symbol representing that particular stimulus.

if an individual's vocal symbol coincides or converges with the similar vocal symbols produced by a number of other members of a community, it becomes a common coinage and circulates as common currency in the consciousness and practice of an entire community. if two or more symbols contend for evoking a similar image and representing a similar object, they become heteronyms, which is why there are two or more names for the same object and two or more distinct objects are referred to by the same vocal symbol in the same language, homonyms.

are speech symbols instinctive reactions and therefore integrally related to the specific objects they refer to? there is enough evidence to show, not only in a few onomatopoeic words but in a number of the common stock words, that the symbols and what they stand for are integrally connected one way or the other. In most of the languages the name for the female parent contains the sound *m and the name for the male parent contains the sound* **p/b** in the significant parts of the words. it is easy to explain. when the human child begins to recognize the face and joyfully address its more familiar parent, it parts its lips to allow the air to pass through both oral and nasal passages, the result being a distinct *m* sound, preceded or followed by an indistinct vowel sound and when it affectionately recognizes the face and addresses its male parent, it momentarily blocks its nasal passage, when parting the lips, the result being a distinct *p* sound, preceded or followed by an indistinct vowel sound. the child, no doubt, is naming its parents. it is no coincidence that languages spoken in regions as far apart as england and china have similar words for mother and father. some common verbs like **come, go, give, take** and common pronouns like **i, you, this, that** and common adverbs like **here, there, now, then** indicate the direction to or away from the speaker. because we cannot find the initial reason for the origin of words, we cannot conclude that the symbols and the images that are recalled to the active folder of the brain by the symbols and their referents in the physical or psychological world are purely arbitrary. (saussure) arbitrary is the relationship between a word and its meaning, at present, what with the innumerable changes the stock words have undergone through the ages in their phonetic, morphological and semantic structures, on the one hand, and the deliberate creation and borrowing of new words.

the bottom line of the present argument is that speech is not species—specific. holding on to the theory that language is species-specific amounts to admitting the pre-evolution of the species' unsustainable ideas through the back door. but specific are the circumstances and the conditions that led to the invention of speech. further it is the instinct which we share with all life around us and emotion but not intelligence with which we are endowed which is at the root and development of all languages. in actual fact intelligence is the product of the continuous mediation between active consciousness of an individual and that of its counterparts in a community through speech. in other words instinct gets converted to emotion and emotion to intelligence through the medium of language. the intelligence, likewise through constant practice gets stored in the acquired or secondary instinct of an individual.

how does a child acquire a particular operating system, a particular language? it is easy to answer. it acquires a language through observation and imitation. but the larger question is why the human child alone can acquire a language. according to chomsky, universal grammar is wired into its brain before it is born. learning and practicing a language contribute to a large extent for the increase and development of the brain. the hardware configuration improves from generation to generation. and most importantly the capacity and power of the active memory which is essential for acquiring a language increases enormously. even an average human child has a larger active memory than a well-developed chimpanzee, which is why a human child can acquire a language and a chimpanzee cannot. the active memory is also necessary for doing even simple sums, equations and puzzles. the larger active memory, ram, enables a person to keep more and more bits of information floating in the brain so that the needle of the mind can toggle between one point and another in all directions to order the suspended bits of information into a tangible and sensible pattern. the size of the active memory is the measure of all intelligence and it is the active memory which effortlessly delves deep into the passive memory and draws the necessary bits of information for the present purpose. to quote einstein, undoubtedly one of the greatest thinkers of the twentieth century, *"it is not that i am smart it is just that i stay with problems longer."* no universal grammar is required to be wired into the brain to acquire language skills but a larger active memory than is present in all other species is what is required to frame sentences, quite a number of which can be reduced to simple mathematical equations.

a language which separates humankind from all other life around it also, to a considerable extent, determines and limits its intellect, which is why a human child should be given an opportunity to learn at least one more language other than its native language, particularly, a language spoken by a community living in a different cultural milieu than its own, in order to liberate itself from being enslaved by its native language. we cannot make ourselves totally free from the structure of genes in which we were encapsulated before birth. similarly we cannot liberate ourselves from the tyranny of the languages we speak until and unless we simplify them and adapt them to our present needs. in other words, we must needs jettison a lot of dead weight which goes under the prestigious, in the opinion of some people and opprobrious, in the opinion of some others, name of grammar, in order to overcome the limitations imposed on our minds by language.

like any other tool or product, a language must be made user-friendly. and by the by, we can also save ourselves a good deal of needless litigation and altogether avoidable verbal controversies that rage between spokespersons of the powerful political parties and the members of the influential fourth estate if the languages are made more simple and less problematic.

Languages need to be made simple, plain and rational for another reason. As the children have to learn subjects, including mathematics, through the medium of a language, English or regional, we can spare them from the arduous task of struggling with the complicated and convoluted structures of the present day languages.

it is high time we determined the shape and structure of our languages for yet another important reason. computers have not only come to stay but they have also become indispensable at present. we have the challenging task of achieving a total interface with the intelligent machines. one part of doing it is making the machines more intelligent. our computer scientists [a I experts] have made considerable progress in this direction. nevertheless, it is not enough. the other part of our task is making our languages more computer-friendly. they should be made more simple, straightforward and more efficient systems of communication.

CHAPTER 1

word classes

a grammar of a language, besides being internally consistent, needs to encompass and interpret all the possible structures of that language. a grammar needs to formulate rules which are based on standard practice in the spoken and written varieties of that language or are tested in the crucible of their practical application. it should also find out those structures which are peculiar to that language and those which it shares with other languages so that we can formulate a plausible theory of a grammar common to all languages, living or dead.

the traditional grammar, interpreting structures primarily on the basis their meaning, recognizes eight classes of words, called parts of speech, including interjections. but interjections cannot be classified as words or phrases. they are, in fact, clauses or sentences by themselves. as per the present day classification which is based on position, function and form rather than on the meaning of structures, there are eight classes of words.

there are three classes in group (a), **nouns, pronouns** and **adjectives.**

class one words are naming words**, nouns,** used to identify persons, animals, things, ideas etc. it is an open set of words absolutely necessary for any verbal communication. nouns are a universal set. traditional grammar divides nouns into as many as five classes, namely, common, proper, collective, material and abstract nouns. this classification has little practical use. the present day grammar divides all nouns, broadly, into two classes, namely, **countable** and **uncountable**. ex. b**ook, boy** etc. are countable whereas **milk, iron** etc. are uncountable. the nouns belonging to the former class, unlike those belonging to the latter class, have plural forms and can be modified by both the indefinite article and the definite article in their singular forms and by the definite article only in their plural forms. the uncountable can be modified by the definite article only. ex. b**ook—a book, the book, and the books**: boy—**a boy, the boy, the boys** but not **milks*, irons*, a milk*, an iron*** but **the milk, the iron**.

as nouns are an open set, new nouns are continuously added to this set, either created internally or borrowed from other languages. one important source from which new nouns are drawn is verbs. verbs and their active participle forms are converted to nouns if there are no corresponding nouns denoting the particular activity. ex. b**eat, meet, feed, beating, meeting and feeding**. sometimes the active participle forms are converted to full nouns with their own plural forms. ex. **greeting(s), bearing(s), reading(s) booking(s)** etc. infinitives and active participles of verbs function as nouns, naming activities denoted by the verbs. ex. r**eading makes a full man**. **to err is human**.

verbs, adjectives, adverbs, prepositions and conjunctions are suffixed to form nouns. ex. a**ction (from act), statement (from state); goodness (from good), honesty (from honest); nowness (from now), nowadays; ins and outs; ifs and buts** etc.

nouns are borrowed, with remarkable facility, from other languages. ex. **bandit is borrowed** from italian, **kindergarten** from german, **buffet** from french, **ahimsa** from sanskrit and **bandicoot** from telugu **horde** from urdu. **n**ouns modify other nouns to form **noun compounds**. **a** s**teel bureau, a problem child** (noun compound. noun + noun.) can be expanded as **a bureau made of steel, a child who is a source of problems for adults taking care of it**. **i**ndian american, engineer **entrepreneur, animal lover, goods train** etc. active and passive participles join nouns to make compounds. ex. **finishing touches, training camp** can be expanded to avoid any possible ambiguity or confusion as "**adding 'the final improvements so that you are satisfied with it or you are certain that it is complete.**"(*CALD)*, **a camp where training is given to persons for a particular job.**

compound nouns are different from noun compounds. the former are formed by compounding nouns with other nouns or verbs with other classes of words to create single words, hyphenated or

2

not. **ex. book-worm, windmill, windfall, taxpayer bath-tub** (noun+noun), **wash-basin, haircut, cut-throat heartbeat, walking-stick, washing-machine, air-conditioning, note-taking** (active participle+noun) **sit-in, make-up, lock—up, stand-by, mix-up**(verb+adparticle)

the class two words are pronouns, words, used instead of nouns [in actual fact, it is nouns which are used instead of pronouns], an entirely closed set of stock words, as old as the language itself. It has a subset called personal pronouns. Personal pronouns are also a universal set. they are **i, we, you, he, she, it** and **they.**

the words of class **three** are **adjectives**, words, used to describe the quality or quantity of nouns. it is an open set of words. new adjectives usually come from nouns and verbs and sometimes from other languages. adjectives normally precede nouns and modify them to form simple noun phrases (modifier+ head word). adjectives do not modify pronouns as they refer to persons or things already identified. adjectives are used only attributively in south Indian languages but they can be used as independent complements or as parts of predicates in english and Hindi. ex. **blue sky, comfortable chair. the sky is blue. the chair is comfortable.** In fact, t**he chair is comfortable** is a brief construction derived from the kernel construction, **the chair is a comfortable chair.** (**the second noun, chair is dropped as it has already occurred in the** sentence and consequently the article **a** is also dropped to construct a brief structure.**)**

this shows that processing of meaning is easier when the adjectives precede nouns and not the other way about**.** adjective+ noun is a normal and universal feature. noun+adjective is a derived feature cultured by versifiers for the exigencies of rhyme and rhythm and cultivated by pundits as a mark of sophistication. this order is rarely found in english except in a few set phrases, which are actually translations from other languages like french. ex. **palace royal**. the words, **astir, afraid, astride** etc, used only predicatively, are classified as adjectives but they function more like adverbs than adjectives. ex. s**he is afraid of cockroaches**.(she is in fear of cockroaches) adjectives **trendy, beautiful, industrious, running, damaged** are derived from **trend, beauty, industry, run** and **damage** respectively. nouns can modify adjectives to form adjective compounds, which, however, is not a very productive feature. ex. **sky-blue, purse-proud** etc adjectives have a closed sub-set of pro-words, **a, an, the,** called articles, **this, these, that and those** called demonstrative adjectives.

a subset of pronouns and adjectives is **determiners/determinatives,** which include [a] articles, **a {an}** and **the,** [b]demonstrative adjectives/ pronouns, **this, that, such,** possessive adjectives/pronouns, **my. mine Our, ours, your, yours, his, his, her, hers, its, its, their and theirs** distributive adjectives/pronouns, **each, either, neither every/everyone** and adjectives determining a definite or indefinite number or amount such as **no/none, nothing, nobody, any/anyone/anybody, one, two etc, some, little, much, few many** etc. the determiners/determinatives are defined by some linguists as words forming a separate set because they point out nouns without describing them and precede all other adjectives in a noun phrase. 'a determiner indicates a function, a determinative a class.' 'a determinative is another word for a determiner' [c o d] a determiner is pronominal and a determinative is adjectival. **all, both** and **half** are determinatives in british English. example: **all** the boys, **both** the teams, **half** his wealth [determinatives] (br) **all** of the boys, **both** of the teams and **half** of his wealth [determiners] (american). **little** and **few** take articles as pre—modifiers in all varieties of english. the linguists classify determiners and determinatives as a separate class and then further divide them into articles, possessives etc, which is an exercise in futility, coining new words yet adding little to further any understanding of the language, all of which shows that mostly researches in humanities are like efforts, amounting to digging an entire mountain to catch a little inconvenient rat.

group (B) consists of a single class of words, class **four** words, **verbs,** words, used to describe a status, an action etc of nouns or pronouns functioning as subjects. it is an open set as most nouns can be used as verbs. a verb or a verbal phrase forms the nuclear element of a clause or a sentence. (the number of verbs or verbal phrases is equal to the number of clauses.) verbs have two closed sub-sets, the primary auxiliaries (**be, do, have**) and the modal auxiliaries (**will, can** etc) group (c) consists of class **five** words, **adverbs or adverbials**, words or phrases, used to modify verbs. adverbs have a closed sub-set of pro— words, **here, there, now, then, so** and **thus**. the main set of adverbs is derived from adjectives through -ly suffixation. ex. **full <fully, loving<lovingly**. but the present trend is to use adjective forms as adverbs as well. first second etc full, easy have joined the ranks of **hard, fast, little** etc, words used as adjectives and adverbs. this is a welcome and progressive trend as the position of such words determines their function as is the practice in chinese the third set of adverbials is prepositional phrases. (preposition+noun/noun phrase) ex. **on the table, in the hall etc**.

the class **six** words are **intensifiers** which were once classified as adverbs. these words are used to intensify or give force or emphasis to adjectives or adverbs. ex. **very, right, exactly, hugely** etc.(1) he is not here **right** at the moment.(2) she is **hugely** popular with the students.(3) the child is **too** tall for its age. (4) they are running **very** fast. most of the intensifiers function as adverbs as well. the plant is **fully** operational. (intensifier) he hasn't comprehended the text **fully**. (adverb) some intensifiers do not function as adverbs. he parked the car **right** in front of the gate. he behaved **very** indecently with his wife in full public view. some hollywood films are **hugely** successful in india.

the difference between an intensifier and an adverb is in its position and not in its form. the position of the intensifier is fixed, that is, right before the adjective or the adverb it intensifies while the adverb can be moved to other positions in a sentence. ex. it is a **richly** endowed award. (intensifier. its position is fixed.) she **richly** deserves the award. **richly** does she deserve the award. (adverb) she deserves the award **richly**. (adverb). intensifiers have a closed sub-set in **so, such** and **as**.

group (d) consists of two classes, class **seven**, **prepositions** and class eight **conjunctions.**

prepositions such as **in, on, at, by, for, until, worth, absent** etc. are used before nouns or pronouns (a) to form adverbial phrases in a sentence or (b) to form qualifiers in noun phrases. they are also used after verbs to form phrasal verbs in which case they can be called adparticles ex. the newspaper is **on the table in the hall**. (adverbial phrase) the newspaper

on the table in the hall is yesterday's (qualifier) he is **putting on** airs. (phrasal verb, verb +adparticle). the adparticles also bond with adjectives and adverbs. ex. **good at, known for, afraid of.** these particles combine with verbs and their active and passive participles and nouns to form new words. **ex. Sit-in, back-up, on-going, in-fighting, in-built, in-depth.** etc.

conjunctions, [in fact, most of them are a subset of adverbs] purely functional words, are used to join words, phrases or clauses of the same class [coordinating conjunctions or linkers] such as:—**and, but, or, so** or words used to join dissimilar clauses [subordinating conjunctions or clause markers] such as, **that, because, though, if, whether, when, now that, once, the moment** etc. conjunctions and prepositions have a common set in the words such as **before, after, till, until, for** etc. **once, the moment** and **now that,** which are primarily adverbs, are used as conjunctions. ex. <u>once</u> **you become a popular film star, you lose a great deal of your privacy, for you are constantly in the gaze and scrutiny of the public.**(the kernel expression is **when once. when** is dropped, **once** assuming the function of a conjunction.) **the moment i saw him i recognized him**. (the kernel phrase is **at the moment when) now that his book store in chennai is doing good business, he intends setting up similar book stores in all the other major cities in india.** (the kernel construction is **as now)**

as words and phrases frequently change classes, it is their position and the class of words that associate with them and not normally their forms that indicate their class. consider the following examples:-

- (a.) we d**emand** your explanation. (b.) the **demand** for food items, being high, food prices are soaring in the world market. **demand** in (a.) is a verb as it is in the second element of the sentence. the same word in (b) is a noun as it constitutes the first element of the sentence and also because it is preceded by a modifier in the form of **the.** (a.) He runs **fast.** (b.) it is a **fast** train. (**fast** is an adverb in sentence (a), because it constitutes an independent element, adverbial and the same word is an adjective, a dependent word forming part of a noun phrase in the sentence (b.) we have **enough** food in the fridge (adjective). please be kind **enough** to join us. (intensifier) you haven't **fully**

6

comprehended the meaning. (adverb). the machinery will be **fully** operational from next week.(intensifier) wait here **until** the train arrives. (clause marker). wait here **until** the arrival of the train. (preposition). you must be present here **before** the meeting commences.(clause marker) you must be present here **before** the commencement of the meeting. (Preposition) the **running** time is an hour and a half.(active participle used as an adjective,) the train is **running** two hours late.(the lexical verb is used in the active participle form.) the **running** of trains on this track is suspended after an accident. (verbal noun or gerund)

position of a word or a phrase in a sentence

unlike in most other languages, it is the position that determines the function, the form and the meaning of structures in english, which is why english is more computer—friendly than most other languages.

nouns and pronouns normally occur in the first, third or fourth element position in a sentence. adjectives normally precede nouns to form noun phrases. verbs occur in second element position to form verbal phrases.

adverbs and adverbial phrases, normally placed at the end of a sentence, round off sentences, tying up the noun phrase with the verbal phrase or tying up the entire sentence as one meaningful unit or tying up the total discourse in a logical or sequential bind.

we will take a polysemic word, **fast** and process its form, function and meaning from its position. there is now a **fast** train to delhi. (an adjective, placed before the noun, **train.**) the car is running very **fast. (a**n adverb, placed at the end of the sentence, preceded by an intensifier) they **fast** from sunrise to sunset.

(a verb, placed in the second element position.) an occasional **fast** is good for health. (a noun, placed in the first element position, preceded by an article and an adjective) uneducated people always hold **fast** to their superstitious beliefs. (an adverb, meaning firmly)

exercise 1. name the class to which the words in the following passages belong. (adj. = adjective, adv. = adverb, art. = article, [a, an, the], infn.

= infinitive[infinitive marker 'to' and base form of the verb] intens. = intensifier, noun, prep. = preposition pron. = pronoun, poss.Pron. = possessive pronoun,

- "The greatest of all cosmological scientific puzzles confounding all our efforts <u>to comprehend</u> it, is the earth.
- We are only now beginning <u>to appreciate</u> how strange and splendid it is, how it catches the breath, the loveliest object afloat around the sun, enclosed in its own bubble of atmosphere, manufacturing and breathing its own oxygen, fixing its own nitrogen from the air into its own soil, generating its own weather." Lewis Thomas in *Discover.*
- "The earth is the wonder of the universe, a unique sphere". *The Earth.*
- "The earth is unique among all the known planets, because it has a breathable atmosphere and water on its surface. This allows life to exist almost everywhere, from the desert sands to the deepest oceans". *Earth and Space*

exercise 2.expand the noun compounds and compound nouns. ex. camp fire= an outdoor fire made at a tent away from homes. cooking apples=apples suitable for cooking only and not suitable for eating raw. bench-mark="something that can be measured and used as a standard that other things can be compared with" *OALD*

repair shop, boarding school, technocrat administrator, beauty parlor, drinking-water, living—room, gift horse, driving school, water-tank, car-park, income tax, gas station, memory power, product details, wonder kid, motor engine, cash crunch, driving license, laughing stock, listening device, leave application, lending library, in-service training interest-free loan, cash counter, work permit desk, refill gas cylinder, degree holder and airport lounge.

CHAPTER 2

personal pronouns

In search of a second person plural form

in english and in all the north indian languages there is only one 1ˢᵗ person plural form. the south indian languages, more pronouncedly telugu, have two forms, one, inclusive of the person addressed and the other exclusive. when one says *we* in english there is no way of knowing whether the speaker includes or excludes the person addressed. the additional form in telugu resolves the ambiguity. **we** is being used in some dialects as second person exclusive and **we-all** as second person inclusive.

similarly, there is a problem with the 2ⁿᵈ person plural in english. this is the result of a social tendency of using second person plural as an honorific singular and later extending it to any singular second person, the actual singular form **thou** totally disappearing as a consequence. the mutation, namely, the gradual disappearance of **thou**, without any compensatory device to resolve the ambiguity, has rendered not only English but also many Indian languages deficient in this respect. as a result, the plural form is now used for both singular and plural in english. to resolve this ambiguity, **you** is being used for singular and the form **you-all** is being adopted as the plural form in some southern u s dialects.

except *you* and *it,* all other personal pronouns have two forms, one used in the subject position and the other used in the object position or after a preposition. In fact, the same form can be used in both the subject and object positions as the position determines the function in english. however, the subject form, being a stressed form, is used in the 1ˢᵗ position and the oblique form is used in the third position, whether the

9

pronoun functions as a complement or an object, quite justifiably, in the spoken variety.

examples: (1} it's **me**. (2) he is taller than **me**. but" he loves her more than **i** do."(the sentences (1) and (2) are considered ill—formed by purists. using **i** in the place of **me** makes the sentences well-formed, according to them.

unlike in most indian languages, there is no reflexive pronominal possessive particle in english. **Own,** used after the possessive, does not adequately serve the purpose, functioning more as an intensifier than as a reflexive particle. example:-

he got married to his cousin. (he got married to whose cousin? he married some other person's cousin or his own cousin. [ambiguous])

he got married to his own cousin. (**he** got married to whose cousin? he got married not to someone one else's cousin but to his own cousin. **[needless emphasis]**)

either too little or too much emphasis is placed by the intensifier **own** but the point is entirely missing. the reflexive particle is used in the place of 3rd person possessive to resolve the ambiguity in south indian languages whereas it is needlessly used in the places of 1st and 2nd personal possessives as well in hindi. in non-standard spoken hindi it is also used in place of 1st person pronoun.

forms of personal pronouns

	Subject	*Object*	*possessive adjective*	*possessive pronoun*	*reflexive or emphatic*
first person singular	*I*	*Me*	*My*	*mine*	*Myself*
first person plural	*We*	*Us*	*Our*	*ours*	*Ourselves*
second person singular	*You*	*You*	*Your*	*yours*	*Yourself*

second person plural	You	You	Your	yours	Yourselves
third person singular	He	Him	His	his	Himself
	She	Her	Her	hers	Herself
	It	It	Its	its	Itself
third person plural	They	Them	Their	theirs	Themselves

possessive adjectives are totally dependent class of words which are used only attributively before nouns or noun phrases whereas possessive pronouns function as nouns. ex. this is **his** book. **his** is unstressed.) this book is **his**. (**his** is stressed.) **she is one of my aunts**. an aunt of **mine** is visiting us this afternoon. possessive nouns function as adjectives also. this is ravi's uncle. this is an uncle of ravi's. (**this is an uncle of ravi** is equally unambiguous but on the analogy of pronouns, the possessive noun is preferred.)

personal pronouns do not take defining qualifiers or defining relative clauses as particular persons or things need not be defined again. but **he,** used as an indefinite pronoun like **one** is an exception. **he** who lives and let s others live **lives** happily. (well-formed). **they** who live in glass houses should not throw stones. (ill-formed). we have to use **those** instead of **they.** a reflexive pronoun is used as object when the subject and the object refer to the same person or thing. ex. **he injured himself**. but mostly it is used for emphasis. ex. **i did it myself**. (i did it by myself without anyone's help.) **the boss himself came here to share the joyful news with you**. (he did not send anyone to convey the news to you. he himself did come.)

exercise 3.

fill in the blanks by using the appropriate alternatives given in the brackets.

* this is _____ umbrella. this umbrella is _____ (my, mine.)
* it is _____ house. this house is _____ (hers. her.)

- this gentleman is the brother of _____.(abdullah, abdullah's.)
  a brother of _____ is in the u. s.(abdullah, abdullah's)
- this institution is _____.
  please visit _____ institution.(our. ours)
- when are you going to _____ village? _____ is a small hamlet near madurai.(their, theirs)

exercise 4. correct the following sentences replacing the ill-formed words with well formed words and resolve the ambiguity, if any.

- her sister is not as industrious as her.
- i cannot walk faster than him.
- she who is in a green frock is a niece of kumar's
- it is them, who knocked at your door, not me.
- my wife loves our children more than me.
- it's me. i want to talk to you.
- my brother and myself went to school together.
- he injured his own self while doing exercises.

CHAPTER 3

nouns and their plural forms

sanskrit nouns have three numbers, singular, dual and plural, three irrational genders masculine, feminine and neuter, making the language difficult to learn, giving, all the same, no specific advantage to it as a communication system. chinese nouns remain unchanged, when denoting plural number as well and chinese is not any the less effective for that. japanese nouns, except for a handful of them, denoting human beings, have no plural forms. near home, in spoken tamil, plural forms of nouns are rarely used except when referring to adult human beings. in actual fact, plural forms of nouns do not add to the accuracy or efficacy of communication. denoting definite or indefinite quantity of nouns is the domain of adjectives. it is all the more necessary to dispense with the plural forms of english nouns for the following among the grounds:-

material nouns do not change their forms: ex. **iron, water, mutton, sand, food** etc. some nouns, though quite a few, do not have separate forms for plural.ex. **sheep, deer, salmon** etc. nouns, functioning as adjectives are used only in their singular forms when denoting a plural quantity as well. Ex. **trouser pockets, Two dozen chairs, two score apples, three hundred men** etc. besides, we use singular forms in phrases with *type, kind* etc as in *types of plant, kinds of sentence*. *there is a progressive tendency to drop the plural suffix*

making matters much worse, the suffix **s** has three different duties to perform. it indicates [1] a plural noun, [2] a possessive adjective preceded by an apostrophe mark in written variety and [3] the 3rd person singular tense form of a verb. example: **three cooks, cook's salary and cooks' salaries. she cooks lunch**. besides, indicating both a plural noun and a singular form of a verb sounds quite paradoxical for a learner with no notion of the development of the english language.

to further confound the confusion, there are some most commonly used nouns, which have irregular plural forms, making unnecessary demand on the time of the young learners. examples: **man—men, woman—women, child—children, ox—oxen, foot—feet, goose—geese, mouse—mice, louse—lice.**

there is yet another altogether retrogressive practice which is against the grain of english. When borrowing nouns from latin, the plural forms are needlessly imported along with their singular forms. as better sense prevails now, ***stadiums, syllabuses*** are preferred to ***stadia*** and ***syllabi.***

besides, adding a plural suffix necessitates complicated morphological changes in the forms of some nouns such as **leaf—leaves, life—lives, church—churches** etc. there is yet another problem when we interface a computer, for there are no fewer than three plural forms in the spoken variety of english, namely, s, z and **iz** for which additional provision is to be made in the speech recognition software.

at present only countable nouns have plural forms. b**ook—books, picture—pictures**. etc. **milk, iron, kindness, furniture, scenery** etc have no plural forms as they are uncountable nouns.

hence, there is a good case for sending the plural suffix (**s, es**) to the recycle bin, at least, for now, if we cannot adopt a standard predictable plural suffix for all countable nouns.

exercise 5.

identify the countable nouns in the following and give their plural forms. speech, means, light, gentleman, man-servant, maid-servant, sister, sister-in-law, roof, scarf, beauty, mystery, grant-in aid, knife, species, phenomenon, bacterium, focus, locus, bench, bus, mess, rajesh, kamala, ganges, himalayas, formula.

exercise 6.

identify the nouns in the following passage and state whether they are countable or uncountable and give their singular/ plural forms, if they are countable.

There's always one smarter than you

not long ago, in fact, this happened quite recently, a monkey, in a pensive mood, was sitting at the water's edge of a river bank. the sweet smell of ripe mangoes, was hitting its nostrils, coming from the orchard on the opposite bank of the river. the river was in full spate since last evening after incessant rains upstream on the far away mountains. he was neither a fish to swim across the river nor a bird to fly over it. he had his last meal two days ago, a dry, half-eaten hard flesh of a coconut fruit.

a crocodile, who read many books on the monkey psychology, swam near the water's edge and said," hi cousin, want any help?" she was also famished and hungry. her last meal was a young trout, all bones and no flesh, which she had to share with her youngest babe. "you want to cross the river and get at the mango grove, don't you? sit on my back and i will stand you on the opposite bank in a jiffy," added the crocodile alluringly.

the monkey thought over the offer and said, "look, lady, i can't trust you. you are a predator and i am a prey. of course, you want to have me for your lunch, i am sure. you can't trick me, i am hungry though." "don't have a fear, young man. we, crocodiles, do not relish monkey's meat. i am in a mood to do some social service. i promise you i won't do no harm to you." "you will do me harm then, no doubt. your words have betrayed your real intentions. freud and jung were my favorite authors at my university, you know." "o me! it's a double negative, i spoke the british idiomatic or idiotic english" chuckled the crocodile. "i will do you no harm. i solemnly promise. rats must be running in your stomach as the telugu people say." "no, mice are running in my stomach,' said the hindi knowing monkey, as he sat astride the crocodile's back, though he sensed danger. we would cross the bridge when we came to it [as the politicians normally say], thought the monkey. at the moment the sweet smell of ripe mangoes was irresistible.

half way across the river, the crocodile turned its head and looked mischievously at first and then menacingly. "stupid monkey, how can you trust your enemies when you can hardly trust even your friends these days? you are going to be my first full meal in nearly three days." "this isn't fair. you made a solemn promise, didn't you?" cried the monkey. "yes," said the monster, i stand by my word, though all is fair in food and war. i have read somewhere that the brain of a monkey tastes awfully good. i'll just eat your brain and leave you unscathed."

when the crocodile started baring its teeth, the monkey hit upon a plan, looked as calm as he could in the circumstances and said, "wait, my friend, i didn't bring my brain with me. what use is a brain when i am simply hunting for food? i kept my brain on the topmost branch of the neem tree where I am put up now, before I undertook the journey. just turn around and see a black leather case hanging from that neem tree, if you doubt my words," "you can't make an owl of me, as they say in the indian official language. the brain is in the skull of an animal, not atop a tree. a monkey's head is in its tail, it is rightly said of monkeys," said the crocodile, taking his time as he was sure that his prey could not escape, however hard he tried. he wanted to have some fun before a hearty meal.

the monkey laughed at him and said," your ideas on anatomy are outdated. living under deep water for so long, you have lost touch with the present day world. you are like a frog living in a well. nowadays you can keep your liver, kidney or even your heart in your palm without any harm. be wise and think well before you rue your hasty action later. i promise I'll retrieve the brain and present it to you and you can still keep your promise to help me cross the river. I'm not losing anything in the bargain. One phone call and 'll get a new brain."

the thick—headed reptile reflected on the matter for one long moment, turned a u-turn and swam back to the shore they had left a few minutes ago. as soon as the crocodile reached the water's edge, the monkey jumped off the back of the monster, stood at a safe distance, grinned, as monkeys normally do, and said to the bewildered crocodile, as he knew he was out of harm's way," "you crooked reptile, how could you believe me when i said my brain was on the branch of a tree? there is only a laptop in that black bag. it is a brain outside a brain. i didn't lie when i said i left my brain on the tree. the computer is like a brain, an external one, it can do complicated sums. it can store vast amounts of information. it can run programs. only thing is you can't eat it. you can't clothe your body with it. you can't even cover your head with it when there is a downpour, which is why some people think it's useless. thank you for a free but very interesting ride all the same. no bitterness and no hard feelings. good evening. happy hunting next time round at least. but remember there can be always one smarter than you." so haranguing, the monkey went back to the tree, leaving the crocodile, stunned and speechless, who beat a fast retreat into the cavern of deep waters to hide her blushes.

CHAPTER 4

adjectives

adjectives in english, as well as in south indian languages, are, to a large extent, a liberated class of words. being a dependent class of words, they lead a stressful life in hindi, as they have to change their shape, size and figure as they precede or follow nouns which are not only number—sensitive but also gender—sensitive, the gender, being for all practical purposes, quite whimsical and also sex sensitive.

we, however, face some minor problems in handling english adjectives. the first problem is with the two demonstrative adjectives which have a strong presence in oral discourses, **this** and **that.** as they do a dual duty, both as demonstrative pronouns and demonstrative adjectives, they have plural forms. we have to use plural forms, if the nouns they qualify are plural nouns, contrary to the normal practice with regard to other adjectives thus:

that tigers is an ill-formed phrase while **those tigers** is a well-formed one.

these apple is an ill-formed phrase and **this apple a** well-formed one.

the sub-set of adjectives, called articles, causes considerable anxiety to the learners of english. the articles are peculiar to english, to which there are no equivalent words in indian languages. the indefinite article **a** or **an** is derived from **one** but it cannot be replaced by **one. i saw a tiger in the zoo** is not the same as **i saw one tiger in the zoo.** in indian languages **one** means an uncertain person or thing that the speaker is going to talk about and it is also used to indicate the number **one.** when clarity is required **only** is used as an intensifier.

an is used before a noun or a noun phrase starting with a vowel sound, or otherwise **a** is used. Whether to use **a** or **an** before such words as **european** or **honest man** can be resolved once the present problematic English spelling is reformed. ex. **a dog** but **an elephant; a brother, a sister** but **an uncle, an aunt; a history, a hotel** but **an hour, an honor; an egg, an italian, an umbrella** but **a european, a university, a useful thing.** as language is basically speech and not writing, it is the pronunciation that determines which variant of the indefinite article is be used.

the definite article **the** is derived from the demonstrative adjective but its usage is quite different. **the** means the particular person or thing already referred to, or going to be referred to, in the immediately following defining qualifier. **this** is the book I bought yesterday. (showing the book) **the** book i bought yesterday is slightly damaged. (the particular book, whether it is present at the moment or not.) an intensifier is used with the demonstrative adjective or demonstrative pronoun or third person pronoun as there is no definite article in Indian languages.

it is curious that we can, when referring to a class of animals other than man, use the definite article, the indefinite or plural form of a noun. ex. **a cow is a domestic animal. the cow is a domestic animal. cows are domestic animals.**

there are also elaborate and complex rules, to provide a happy hunting ground for a school teacher ever eager to look for bloomers, while making his puzzled pupils not a bit wiser for all that, concerning where to use and where to omit articles. the following rules, for example, make little sense while requiring a lot more care on the part of the user. but one has to follow these rules if one wants one's english to be proper and impeccable.

(a) don't use any article before school, college, church, temple or mosque when someone visits for learning, praying etc and use one or the other article when one visits those places to meet a friend or get a wedding solemnized. (b) use the definite article before the names of rivers, oceans etc. before unique things such as earth, sun etc., the noun phrases preceded by the adjective in the superlative degree. sometimes what is appropriate in british English is inappropriate in the american variety. should we say **it rained all morning**(am.) or **all the morning**? (br.) the rules regarding the use of articles are so conventionalized that it is time we had a fresh look at them and put some amount of flexibility in their usage. the grammar manuals say, "use **a** before little or few, when an amount or number is enough for the moment and the purpose and if it is not enough, omit **a there is a little sugar in my tea** (as there is some sugar in my tea, don't bother to add any more. **there is little sugar in my tea** is the expression we use when we want our tea to be made to our taste. anyhow it is like digging an entire mountain to catch a little rat, isn't it? (or) are we not making a mountain out of a molehill?

the only sensible rule is that we use the definite article **the** when the person or thing is definite both to the speaker and the hearer and we use indefinite article **a** or **an,** when the identity of a person or thing is yet to be established in the mind of the hearer. however, we can bear the following points in mind.

We use **a** or **an** in S V C sentences and their exclamatory equivalents, as we place a person or thing (a countable noun) in a general class. ex. **I am a teacher.** (but **he is the only history teacher in the school.**) **what a cozy room you have here!** (but **the room is very cozy.**)**what a pleasure to meet you!**(but **the pleasure is mine.**) **copper is an element.** (but **the copper from this mine is of the best quality.**)

when we define an instrument or an appliance, we use **a** or **an. a washing machine is an electrically operated home appliance used to clean, rinse and dry clothes.** (but **the washing machine I bought yesterday is an imported one.**) we use **a** or **an** when quoting rates thus: **ten rupees a dozen. five rupees a kilo.** But we can also say **one dozen ten rupees, one kilo five rupees. I'm taking an oral test next week and a written one the week after the next.** (but **the oral test will be easy. i'm bothered about the written test.**) **your brother comes to school regularly.**(He **comes to study.** no article is necessary) But **why did your father come to the school yesterday?** (a visit to the school for a purpose other than to study and so the definite article is necessary.)(**the trains while passing through the tunnel.** (**Slowest** is an adverb. No article is necessary). **the tallest building in the world is WTC.** (**an** adjective in the superlative degree needs the definite article.) **the poor are affected badly by price rise.** (**the** is used before adjectives to refer to the class of persons of the kind described by the adjectives) another problem with adjectives is regarding the construction of comparative and superlative forms. the present practice is to use intensifiers *more* and *most* before the adjectives and adverbs derived from adjectives, which have more than two syllables. For monosyllabic and dissyllabic words there is no uniform practice. For the adjective *simple* we can use either suffixes—**er** and—**est** or intensifiers **more** and **most**, leading to an avoidable confusion. Even monosyllabic words ending with the suffixes sound quite odd.

OALD gives **cuter, freer** as comparatives of **cute** and **free** which sound like **scooter** and **meter**. **more cute** sounds much better. **more neat, more dry, more wet, more moist** and **more free** sound better than **neater, drier, wetter, moister and freer**, albeit the sticklers may cry "foul". this predicament aside, the learner confronts yet another difficulty. There are irregular comparative and superlative forms like **good** or **well, better** and **best; bad or ill, worse** and **worst; little, less** and **least ; far, farther** and **farthest.** this problem can be put to rest if intensifiers are uniformly used before all adjectives and adverbs derived from adjectives, including **fast** and **hard** which function both as adjectives and adverbs.

degrees of comparison

adjectives and adverbs *in one degree can be converted to other degrees.* changing one degree of comparison to another is more an exercise in logic than in grammar. however, some examples showing the mechanism of changing from one degree to another are given below:-

comparative to positive

a is more industrious than b. (Comparative) **b** is at least as industrious as **a.** (positive)

he is not taller than his brother. (Comparative) **his brother is at least as tall as he.** (Positive)

don't split the infinitive is a dictum which is more followed in breach than in observance. (comparative adjective) **don't split the infinitive is a dictum which is not as much followed in observance as in its breach.**(positive)

21

She speaks English better than her elder brother. (comparative adverb) **her elder brother does not speak english so well as she.** (Positive)

superlative to other degrees

x is the most popular teacher in the school. (Superlative) **x is more popular than any other teacher in the school.** (comparative) **no other teacher in the school is so popular as x.**(positive)

mary is one of the tallest girls in the class. (superlative) **mary is taller than most other girls in the class.** (comparative) **very few girls in the class are as tall as mary.** (positive)

semi-comparatives, **prefer, preferable, elder, junior, senior, superior, inferior** are

followed by the preposition **to** and not **than. he was junior to me in the college.**

different is followed by **from** some in varieties of English and **than** in other varieties.

exercise 7.

use **a** or **an** or **the** in the blanks of the following sentences where necessary.

1. what _____ piece of work is man?
2. he is _____ only surgeon in _____ hospital at _____ moment.
3. what _____ honor to receive _____ award from you.
4. _____ rice is _____ cereal grown in south India.
5. _____ most important crop in _____ punjab is _____ wheat.
6. _____ secretary wrote _____ minutes of _____ meeting.
7. watch _____ sky on a cloudless moonless night.
8. you are _____ happy person when you reach _____ end of _____ long journey.
9. _____ iron found in _____ mine is _____ best.
10. i don't have _____ lot of information but I will give _____ little information I have with me.

22

11. add _____ little sugar if you want it to be _____ little more palatable.
12. there are quite _____ few questions the spokesperson evaded answering.
13. we'll not go shopping today. _____ few shops will open on sundays.

exercise 8.

fill in the blanks with **a, an** or **the,** wherever necessary

the teacher: raman, have you ever seen _____ deer?

raman: yes, sir. we went to _____ zoo last sunday, my dad, my mum, my little sister roshini and

i. we saw not one but a number of them. we saw _____ beautiful buck. it had two attractive antlers.

the teacher: latha, it is your turn now. Is it _____ male deer or _____ female deer raman has just described?

latha: no, sir. i've no idea.

gopal: can I answer _____ question, sir, please? the teacher: o k, go ahead

gopal: it is _____ male deer, sir. It is a buck. Only _____ bucks have antlers. does don't have them.

the teacher: you are right. among animals, males and females have different characteristics. in fact, male _____ animals look more beautiful than _____ female animals. among birds also, you see. _____ peacock sports long beautiful blue and green tail feathers as though painted with _____ brush. _____ peahen looks homely in comparison.

raman: even among humans, sir. You have, for instance, _____ fine mustache but the english mis. doesn't _____ (_____ class laughs and the teacher is angry) the teacher: will you shut your bloody mouth up? did I ask you _____ question?. _____ class is dismissed. disperse all of you this very moment.

exercise 9.

give the other degrees.

- the elephant is the largest land animal.
- whales are larger than elephants.
- don't think that you are smarter than others.
- do you think yesterday was warmer than today?
- shimla apples are not so good as Kashmir apples.
- it rains more in forests than in towns and cities.
- that was one of the most tragic incidents I had witnessed in all my life.
- of all the film actors, she is the most popular though not the prettiest.
- it is more prudent to mind one's business than to meddle in any other's matters unasked.
- she doesn't look more cute than her sisters.
- no man can run as fast as a cheetah.
- the reputation of a man rests more on his work than on his ornate speeches.
- nowadays it is not so expensive to buy a new home appliance than to get the old one repaired.
- children are more prone to be affected by viruses than adults.
- what I say now is more important than anything I have said before.

CHAPTER 5

Verbs

while dealing with verbs, we encounter a plethora of problems. verbs have a minimum of three forms and a maximum of eight. forming plural forms of nouns is an altogether mechanical device, the deletion of which does not affect the character of a language, its clarity, expressiveness or efficacy. it is not so with regard to verbs.

The primary auxiliaries **be, do and have** function both as lexical verbs and auxiliaries. ex. A dolphin **is** a mammal. i **did** my home work. he **has** a house in chennai. (lexical) he **is** playing tennis. i **did** not do it. he **has** had his breakfast.(auxiliary). the primary verb **be** has eight forms and **do** and **have,** have five forms each.

be (base form) **am, is, are** (present) **was, were**(past) **being**(active participle) **been**(passive participle.)

do (base form) **do, does**(present) **did**(past) **doing**(active participle) **done**(passive participle.) **have** (base form) **have, has** (present), **having** (active participle), **had** (past and passive participle)

verbs in English have an important syntactical function to perform. they have to separate the grammatical subject from the grammatical object, for which reason, verbs, like in chinese, occur in the second position. mutations may prove detrimental and sometime s even fatal to living organisms as well as to living languages unless compensatory devices are developed or are activated if they are already present. the slow, gradual but inevitable loss of case endings resulted in effecting certain adjustments in the grammatical structure of english. verbs which used to occur normally in the second position in old English are now more firmly fixed in the second position in between the subject and the object in order to separate them as the subject and the object have the same form. now that this device is rendered inadequate in questions, **do** is invested with the new duty of an operator.

because the subject has become not only necessary but compulsory, passive constructions have assumed disproportionately greater importance in order to avoid the altogether redundant or vexatious subject. It is for the same reason that english is a null-subject language in the case of imperative sentences. in order to distinguish imperative sentences from statements, the subject **you** is always omitted.

example: **you go to school regularly**. (ambiguous. is it simple present or imperative?)

go to school. (imperative)

the omission of the subject in the above case has become necessary because verbs have lost their distinct imperative forms. if subject is retained, it has to carry a stronger than normal stress. subject i or **we** is also optional when the object is the second person. example:

thank you. (i or **we** is omitted.)

to make English more simple, the dead weight we have to jettison is the inflexion **s of the plural nouns, the s** of the 3rd person singular verb. example: **he know me well** can be accepted as a well-formed sentence and need not be frowned upon as dialectical or non—standard. **s** will remain the possessive suffix of nouns, rendering apostrophe mark unnecessary. the apostrophe mark can be deleted from the keyboard. the possessive case ending is a universal feature found both in inflectional as well as non—inflectional languages.

but old habits die hard. verbs have got to agree with their subjects in person and number till we drop the only remaining inflection we have in English other than the possessive particle. However, english is less cumbersome and more rational than hindi. The verb, in hindi, has to agree with the subject in gender as well and the gender is arbitray to make the matters much worse.

at present there is an agreement in number and person in the case of the verb **be.** i **am, we are, you are, he is, they are, i was, we were**. Other verbs have only two different forms.

ex. **look, looks. she looks lovelier than her sisters. the buildings look a lot better after yesterday's showers**. there is a feature in hindi which makes it necessary for a male child to learn its language from its male parent and the female child from its female parent. the first person singular verb is sex sensitive, which is a primitive feature somewhat absurdly retained in the present day hindi. however, even in english subject-verb agreement presents quite a few problems, particularly, for a non-native learner of english.

- the verb agrees with the head word and not with its qualifier. ex. o**ne** of my uncles **is** visiting us next week. t**he life-span** of butterflies **is** short. (**one** and **the life-span** are the head words and the actual subjectsand so **is** is used and not **are**.) [in Indian languages, the actual subject(head word) is placed at the end of the noun phrase while in English the qualifiers follow the head word. Hence the Indian learners of english are prone to make mistakes.

- in s v c type sentences the verb agrees with the complement and not the subject. ex. two thousand miles **is** a long distance for anyone to venture travelling in a train.(not **are**) but **nouns are a universal set or nouns is a universal set**?

- sometimes the usage is the guide to follow and sometimes, the meaning. bread and butter **is** fine for a simple breakfast. A number of witnesses **were** examined and cross-examined. (but the number of dead in the recent railway accident **is** fifty.)

- parliament, assembly, army and council are normally considered singular but military is considered sometimes plural. The council **is** meeting to discuss the proposal. the military **was/were** called out to assist the civil authorities in rescue operations in the flood-devastated areas.

- fluency in both Telugu and English is essential.

- every officer and every worker is responsible for the clean maintenance of the plant. (**each** and **every** are treated as singular even when they are joined by and.)

27

- each boy and each girl is to do social service at least two hours a week.
- there is a present for everyone. there are gifts for all of you. (when **there** is the nominal subject, the verb has to agree with the complement.)
- one of my uncles, who is in america, has sent a laptop to me as my birth day gift. (the antecedent of **who** is **one** and not **uncles**)
- rupesh is one of my uncles who have settled in australia. (the antecedent of **who** is **uncles** not **rupesh**)

Exercise 10.

correct the following sentences wherever necessary.

- the pressure of rock and sand change these remains into oil.
- the damages suffered by each and every customer is fully compensated by the company.
- .the wages are paid on the last day of the week.
- a series of earthquakes have hit the island.
- the wages of sin is death.
- mathematics are a difficult subject.
- the power of the waves and wind are used to generate electricity.
- the increase of prices have been attributed to failure of successive monsoons.
- a number of people has lost their houses and property owing to the recent earthquake.
- the number of people who died in the building collapse have increased to ten after one more body is found in the debris.

Exercise 11:

Identify the verbs in the episode that follows

THE CHAIN SNATCHER AND GOD

[the police arrested the chain-snatcher and filed a charge-sheet against him. after fifteen days they took him in a police van and produced him in the court. the trial starts as the judge enters the court hall.]

the judge: Produce the accused. Put him in the dock. What is the boy accused of, prosecutor?

The public prosecutor: your honour, in the broad day light, the accused snatched the gold chain of an aged lady, injuring her in the process, and tried to run away. Two young men, hearing the shrieks of the lady, chased the accused and caught him. They reported the matter to the police, who, reached the crime spot, conducted a preliminary enquiry and filed an f I r. it is an open-and-shut case, your honor. An exemplary deterrent punishment must be given to the guilty person

(the accused, whose name is mani, takes the oath.)

The judge: Do you plead guilty or not guilty?

The boy: Guilty, sir.

(as he has no money to retain a counsel, the judge appoints an advocate to defend him.)

The judge: the public prosecutor says it is an open-and-shut case. What is your defense? The accused also pleaded guilty, what can you say in his defense, Mr. chary?

Defense lawyer: Your honor, every case is an open-and-shut case for our learned public prosecutor. the accused is a mere boy.

The judge: which is why the juvenile court is trying the accused.

D. L: absolutely, your honor. But what about the redeeming circumstances? Nobody commits a crime for fun or as a hobby.

judge: what are the noble reasons for snatching the gold chain of a defenseless poor elderly lady?

D l: the lady is not poor, your honor. The old lady, according to my investigation, had a stint in jail, found and convicted guilty of harassing her daughter-law for dowry.

Judge: that was why he snatched her chain? Are we trying the lady or the boy?

Dl : definitely, we are trying the boy only, your honor. But a former convict's nature should be taken into consideration, who stands as a victim in this crime.

JUDGE: is it in the penal code?

DL: no, your honor, I am sorry. Everything can't be found in the book or acts. The boy is a sincere devotee of lord venkateswara.

J: will that mitigate his crime?

DL: no, your honor. I am merely narrating the circumstances. Before his twelfth class public examination, the boy made a vow to god that he would make a pilgrimage to tirupati and put some money in the temple hundi, besides getting his head tonsured. He passed the examination, securing the required minimum marks, of course. He had no money. He was an orphan, living in an orphanage. In such circumstances, he committed this small offense. He is not a delinquent but first time offender.

Judge:. (addressing the accused) why did you vow that you would put some money in the hundi of god at tirupat?

Mani:. My teacher told me that lord venkateswara was a powerful god and he would give us what we would ask.

Judge:. You believe that some gods are powerful and some gods are less powerful?

Mani:. Yes, sir. That was what our class teacher, hostel warden and temple priest told us, boys.

Judge: did you pass the public examination because of god's help. God would have helped you even if you did not study text books?

Mani: no, sir.

Judge: Mr. chari, your son also took the public examination and passed the examination In the first division, I understand, Did he take a similar oath?

Chari: no, your honor. We don't go to temples. I am a rationalist.

Judge: what do you learn from this, mani? We can pass the examination with distinction, if we don't go to temples and pray to god.

(mani is silent)

Judge: answer my question.

Mani: no, sir. It is not necessary to go to a temple or pray to god. What is necessary is good preparation and hard work. Mere prayers won't help.

Judge: excellent. Do you go to ashtrologers to know your future.

Mani: no, sir.

Judge: why?

Mani: they charge a fortune for their services and I don't have money. Besides, my science teacher told us ashtrology was bunkum.

Judge: what reason does he give for his not believing in astrology?

Mani: the planets, predictions on the movement of which are made, are so far away from us on the earth to influence our character or future. Besides, if they at all influence, they should influence us all in the same way.

Judge: what more did the science teacher say about the planets?

Mani: the sun and the moon are not planets. The sun is a star, of which one of the planets is the earth. The moon is a satellite of the earth. Two planets, which are believed to influence our fortunes, are imaginary planets which have their existence only in the books of the astrologers. Therefore astrology is neither a science nor a self consistent theory.

Judge: now youl know, m. chari that our youngsters are uncut diamonds. (addressing mani) you are not a dunce. On the contrary, you are a bright boy. why didn't you score well in the examinations?

Mani: I was not given time to read the class books by the warden or the class teacher. I have to look after the kids of the warden in the hostel. I am sent on errands by the class teacher. I have no books. The books given to me free by the goernment are taken away from me and given to the nephew of the warden.

Judge: now i appreciate the circumstances in which mani did what he did. We cannot punish the warden or class teacher, who misguided the boy. Now, mani, do you realize that you have committed a crime?

Mani: yes, sir, I do. I regret for what I have done. I won't even think of doing such a thing in future.

Judge: now we will proceed with the formalities of the case.

(the elderly lady, whose chain the accused had allegedly snatched, identified the man. the two young men who had chased the accused and caught him, having heard the shrieks of the victim, identified him

and narrated the whole episode. the public prosecutor examined the witnesses to prove mani guilty of the alleged crime. the defense counsel cross examined the witnesses, calling them to the witness box again and again and tried his hardest to defend the accused. after hearing the arguments

for the prosecution and for the defense, the judge pronounced his verdict thus:.

'i find the accused. mani, guilty of chain snatching. i entirely agree with the Public prosecutor's plea that the crimes of this nature are on the increase in the city and the court should award him the maximum punishment as a deterrent to others like him. But I also agree with the defense lawyer, who pleaded that the court should be lenient to the accused as he is a teen-ager and a first time offender. The boy has also admitted his guilt. He says he committed the said crime to fulfill his promise that he would make a pilgrimage to a temple in Andhra Pradesh and put some money in the hundi of that powerful deity because of whose munificence he had once supposed to have passed his examination. He was totally deluded as he attributed his success in the examination to the intervention of a deity. But his own deity said in Ramayan:

'there is an order in the universe which cannot be changed by any divine power or invoked through any prayer. We should live and act in harmony with that order. The changes wrought by time cannot be reversed by any power. nothing can overcome or overtake time. Even time itself is incapable of being conquered, reversed or overtaken by itself.'

The boy says the hostel warden, the temple priest and his class teacher have told him that without god's help, even hard work will not bear fruit. It is the temple priest's bread and butter to mislead people. But why do the hostel warden and the class teacher, instead of doing their duties, put wrong notions in the minds of the youth that prayers will give them everything and protect them from punishment for perpetrating crimes? As long as this delusion is in the minds of people, the country cannot make any progress. the ignorance of dharma will stall and impede progress. i sentence the boy to be sent to the juvenile reform center where he will spend a year, reading books on dharma or natural laws. He will be free to pursue higher studies through correspondence. All facilities should be extended to him for that purpose. As the boy has admittedly learnt a lesson, the punishment the court has awarded should not be considered as a blemish on his character or as a black mark barring him from holding an honorable and responsible office by his future employers. The court is adjourned to the next working day.'

CHAPTER 6

irregular verbs

learning english is rendered an ordeal because of the so called irregular verbs, once known as strong verbs. except **ought to, must,** and possibly **used to**, verbs have a minimum of two forms [modal auxiliaries like **shall**, for example]. a few verbs [24] have three forms only. If

a verb like **cut** of this group had become a standard verb, english would have been an easy language to learn, hardly losing anything in its character, clarity, expressiveness or efficacy.

the standard english verbs like **walk** have four forms. They present no big problems for a learner, as they have a uniform way of forming their past and passive participle forms. ex. **walk** (base form) **walk, walks** (present) **walked** (past and passive participle) **walking** (active participle) if a new verb joins this class either through class conversion, borrowing or internal creation, it follows the paradigm of **walk.**

the following verbs have joined the ranks of standard english verbs, at least, in the american variety of english and their alternative standard forms are increasingly used in

other varieties, making matters easier somewhat.

1 dream, 2 burn, 3 dwell, 4 smell, 5 learn, 6 spell, 7 spill, 8 spoil 9 bereave, 10 lean, 11 leap 12 kneel, 13 wed. 13 wet, 14 quit, 15 sweat, 16 rid, 17 hew, 18 mow, 19 saw 20 sew 21 shear 22 show, 23 sow, 24 strew, 25 swell, 26 awake and **27 wake**

- irregular verbs are very few in number but they are very frequently used verbs. hence the problem. if all the irregular verbs barring the primary verbs **be, do** and **have** are to be conjugated on the paradigm of either **cut** or **walk**, english will be a lot more easy to learn. **gived, swimmed** used as past tense and passive participle forms of **give** and **swim** may sound odd like the american **dreamed** to the british ears but a long habit will make them far more acceptable, sounding, far more familiar and pleasant than the irregular **gave** and **swam**.
- Alternatively, we can use a single verb, **have,** to carry the tense index, and all other verbs being used in their infinitive forms. Example: **I do speak, I did speak,** I **will speak** etc. a similar process is noticed in spoken telugu. The political class, either not being fluent in the language or disinclined to be specific, is using a single verb, **happen/occur**, to indicate the tense, while all other verbs are being used in their infinitive forms, which is a progressive trend.
- All these and other trends toward simplification of English, in particular, and languages, in general, would have reached their finality, had not universal education, though desirable, not slowed down, hampered, stopped or even reversed them altogether.

anyhow a list of the most commonly used irregular verbs with their past tense and passive participle forms are given below:-1. the following verbs are unchanged in the past andpassive participle forms.

bet, burst, cast, hit, cost, cut, hurt, knit let, put, quit, rid, set, shed, shut, slit, split, spread

the following verbs have the same form for past and passive participle,

bind—bound, bleed—bled, breed—bred, bring—brought, buy—bought, catch—caught, cling—clung, deal—dealt, dig—dug, feed—fed, feel—felt, flee—fled, fight—fought, fling—flung, get—got, grind—ground, hang—hung, hear—heard, hold—held, keep-kept, lead—led, leave—left, lose—lost, mean—meant, meet—met, light—lit, read—read, say—said, seek—sought, sell—sold sit—sat, shine—shone, shoot—shot, sleep—slept, slide—slid, sling—slung, spin—spun, stand—stood, stick—stuck, sting—stung, strike—struck, string—strung, sweep—swept, swing—swung, teach—taught, tell—told, think—thought, weep—wept, win—won, wring—wrung.

the following verbs have different forms in the present, the past and the passive participle. ex. b**ear** (base form and present tense form**) bore** (past) **borne** (passive participle)

get—got—got, gotten, write—wrote—written, Swear—swore—sworn

Beat	Beat	Beaten	Lie	lay	Lain
Begin	Began	Begun	Ride	rode	Ridden
Bite	Bit	Bitten	Ring	rang	Rung
Blow	Blew	Blown	Rise	rose	Risen
Break	Broke	Broken	Run	ran	Run
choose	Chose	Chosen	shake	shook	Shaken
Come	Came	Come	Sing	sang	Sung
Do	Did	Done	Sink	sank	Sunk
Draw	Drew	Drawn	Slay	slew	Slain
Drink	Drank	Drunk	speak	spoke	Spoken
drive	Drove	Driven	Stink	Stank	Stunk
Eat	Ate	Eaten	spring	sprang	Sprung
Fall	Fell	Fallen	Steal	stole	Stolen
Fly	Flew	Flown	Stink	stank	Stunk
Freeze	Froze	Frozen	Swim	swam	Swum
Give	Gave	Given	Take	took	Taken
Go	Went	Gone	Tear	tore	Torn
Grow	Grew	Grown	throw	threw	Thrown
Hide	Hid	hid, hidden	Wear	wore	Worn
Know	Knew	Known	weave	wove	Woven

Exercise 12

: underline the irregular verbs and give their present, past and participle forms in the following narration.

launching of an empire

one summer evening, vidyaranya, a learned brahmin, [in fact, at the time when the momentous events of the following narrative took place, most of the learned men were brahmins.] was passing through a thick jungle. his daughter was married to a temple priest, living in a village situated on the northern fringe of the jungle. he had not visited her for a month. he had another good reason for visiting that village, about which the readers will know in the course of this narrative. The sun having already set, he was nowhere near his destination. suddenly he heard some sounds. first he thought those rustling sounds came from leaves as they happily responded to the caresses of the cool summer evening's breeze. then he saw two dark figures, menacingly approaching him. he trembled from head to foot and uttered, 'who are you? i am a poor brahmin. i am on my way to visit my daughter in vijayanagar. please don't harm me. i have no money or gold.' 'what is it in that bloody bag?' the darker and taller of the two asked the brahmin. but before vidyaranya could open his mouth to reply, the man shouted at his comrade,' de bukka, search his bag, and also his clothes.' as the brahmin stood shuddering, the man who was called bukka completed a thorough search.'nothing much except sweets and a couple of silver coins, ariara anna,' said bukka. 'sweets are for my grand children. You can take them and eat them with my blessings,' said the brahmin. 'we don't eat blessings. alright. why the dickens are you carrying silver coins unless you intend visiting the red light area and presenting the money to a sex worker?' asked ariaran. the brahmin slightly blushed but kept quiet as the bandits referred to the amorous purpose of his visit to vijayanagar. then the bandits blindfolded him and led him into their hut. then they removed the blindfold and ordered him to sit on the floor. the brahmin looked round and found the hut cozy with all creature comforts.

'now that you have seen us, our place and our bags of gold and silver, we have no choice. We have got to silence you,' said ariaran,' 'though we don't want to make our hands bloody,' added the brigand. the brahmin fell at his feet, wept loudly and mournfully begged him to spare his life. he promised in the names of his gods and on the lives of his two wives and a dozen children that he would never betray them. the bandits had a long dialogue in a cocktail of tamil, kannada and telugu, regarding how to dispose his prayer or dispose of his dead body. vidyaranya, who knew only telugu, took courage and said, 'i am an astrologer. please, kindly let me return to my village. i have a large family. my family depends on my earnings. i will be of help to you some way or other.' 'how will you help us? you are a poor brahmin yourself,' said bukka, the younger bandit. 'arey bukkaraja, there is tenderness in your royal look and softness in your words. harihararaja, I think, that must be your good name, there is majesty in your gait. i see royalty in your faces.' 'you are a base flatterer. you will bring disaster and death to us if we don't do you in.' said hariharan.'

'please believe me. i have a grand plan for you both. tell me about

yourselves first, I think you are brothers, aren't you? 'asked the

brahmin. 'in a way. we were born to the same woman; our fathers are different though.' said bukka, in whose eyes the brahmin saw a little gleam of kindness.' In my vision I see a great hindu empire and you will be founders of that empire. you have immense wealth in those bags of gold and silver enough to launch an empire. I have a grand strategy,' said the brahmin, as he waxed eloquent, sensing hope of escape.'

'what is indu?' the brigands asked in one voice, for they haven't heard the word before.' 'if you are not a muslim, a sikh, a buddhist or a christian, you are a hindu,' explained the brahmin, who himself had no notion about it. well, tell me about yourselves, my noble princes.' then the bandits told their story thus.

they were the sons of a mathaliyar woman, who married a telugu naidu. when her son, hariharan was one year old, she started an illicit affair with a kannada reddiyar. one full moon night, as they were caught by her husband, their mother and her paramour murdered naidu and secretly buried his dead body. ten years after bukka was born, their mother left her paramour and the two children and eloped with a velama dora. the last time the brothers heard about their mother, she was living with a muslim youth, who was young enough to be her son."this is the very stuff from our great epics," said vidyaranya,

'i am an astrologer. I mean people thnk so. they will believe anything and everything i say. my word is an oracular truth for the credulous masses. I hate the masses. when I give fine education to their children,

they give me a pittance for my efforts. i will take now, with your help, a new avatar as a god man. like your royal selves, I am also a crossbreed. my brahmin mother made a cuckold of her husband and had an amorous affair secretly with a gouda landlord, my biological father.'

'you too are a bloody bastard like us,' said hariharan. 'we are all bastards, harihara raja. man is a bastard, if he is anything. we are not primary or secondary bastards but enthnary bastards. no race, caste or community is pure. our great epic mahabharat is the story of kingly bastards, aesthetically told by a saintly bastard. Well, you said lord bukka' s royal father was philandering with your mother under the moonlight and your mother had sexploits in full moon nights; therefore you are the descendents of the moon, like pandavas or kauravas. the night is still young. we will discuss the details by and by. you hate your step father, a muslim, don't you? we are launching a hindu empire to be a bulwark against muslim aggression, to be known as vijayanagar empire. You are robbing the people in the cover of darkness illegally and immorally, as bandits, I mean, according to the masses. hereafter, you both as rulers and i as a god man fleece the masses legally and morally as their so called protectors. that serves them right, the harebrained good for nothing masses, ahha hha haa' so saying, the brahmin burst into a hilarious laughter'. 'I will make you kings. There will be a world conqueror [bhuvanavijetha] in your glorious dynasty. If i am not wrong. that pot over there contains sura. prince bukka, please bring the pot here. We will celebrate the occasion fittingly.' 'that is toddy,' said bukka. 'yes, it is called 'sura' in Sanskrit, a divine drink, fit to be offered to gods in a sacrificial fire. that actually made our gods what they are, immortals' said the learned Brahmin, already inebriated by looking at the toddy pot.

thus an empire was launched and the rest of the story you can read in the book, called 'the true history of south india,' the result of the

painstaking efforts of a number of distinguished historians.

CHAPTER 7

causative verbs

in search of causative verbal structures

there are devices in languages spoken in regions as far apart as turkey and Japan to covert intransitive verbs to transitive verbs and transitive verbs to causative verbs by effecting suitable alterations in their stems. This feature is available, to a limited extent, in classical sanskrit and in most of the north indian languages. this is a very productive feature in south indian languages.it is such an enormously productive feature in telugu as almost any base form of the intransitive verb can be altered to be converted into a transitive verb and the same can be converted into first causative, second causative and so on, subject to reasonableness and manageability.

in English we have two pairs of verbs to suggest that a similar causative process was once prevalent. **rise** is intransitive and **raise** is transitive. Similarly, we have **lie** and **lay**.

but on closer scrutiny we find that **rise** and **raise** came into English from different sources, one from anglo-saxon and the other from norwegian. but the members of the second pair can be traced to the same source, which implies that causative device was at work at one time. This inadequacy is real and not imaginary as can be shown by the frequent use of verbs such as **sit, stand** and **walk** in their causative sense. ex. he **sat** the cup on the table. he **stood** me in front of himself in the queue.he **walked** the dog every morning. the verbs **sat, stood** and **walked** are not used transitively in the sense of **put** or **place** but causatively in the sense of **made to sit** and made to **stand** and **made to walk.** The process may be mistaken as transitivization. it is, in fact, causativization. The passive constructions for the above sentences are 'the cup was made to sit on the

41

table, I was made to stand in front of himself and the dog was helped to have a walk' and not 'the cup was sat on the table' etc.

what advantages does this morphological process give to a language? for one thing, it can be a productive feature, facilitating its users to internally create new words. second, as the new words closely resemble their base words, they can be stored easily in the brain through the logical process of association. third, the causative verbs, derived through this process are neutral and color-insensitive in their meanings, which is a real gain.

the intransitive verb **die** has a transitive equivalent verb in **kill**, whereas in languages like hindi, the transitive verb is derived from the intransitive verb thus:—marna—(to die) maarana—(to kill)

there are a few verbs in English which are used both intransitively and transitively. ex. **sell, grow, run, wake, fly** etc. It is still a productive feature, to a limited extent, as we can occasionally use an intransitive verb as a transitive verb and vice versa whenever we cannot find a suitable verb. the verb "**learn**" in the sentence 'I learnt him english' is misconstrued as used in the sense of "**teach**" in non—Standard English, and it is considered vulgar by the proponents of prescriptive grammar. in fact it is used in the sense of 'had a person learn him english', with a causative meaning.

however, there is no device in english to convert, morphologically or otherwise, verbs into causative verbs. this deficiency is made up, though not adequately, by the use of **make, have** and **help** before the base forms of the verbs without the infinitive marker **to** between them. the semi passive construction 'i got the project finished by employing more workers' also is partly a causative construction. All this proves that a mechanism was at work to fulfill the need but it was not carried out to its proper finesse. thus causative construction with a neutral meaning is beyond the reach of English and all other European languages.

as **eat** has a causative verb in **feed**, there is a proper expression as in **she fed the baby with her milk.** Or much better **she breastfed the baby.** We are not constrained to use the clumsy causative verbal phrase **she made the baby drink her milk** and much worse construction **she helped the baby drink her milk. see** has a causative in **show** and we have two meaningful constructions, **I showed him the book, I made him see reason**. but with most other verbs we have no choice but to use a causative construction into which a shade of meaning or color not intended by the speaker creeps in. ex. **i made him learn his lessons; i made him finish the work in time.** the unintended intrusive color is avoided in languages where a productive causative device is available.

there is another set of verbs in south indian languages, which have many innovative devices for clarity and expressiveness. they are the verbs morphologically derived from the stems of some verbs to express the meaning of the subject performing an action for himself/herself.

- **(a} i cooked me some breakfast.**(unclear) (b) **i cooked some breakfast for myself.**
  (needless emphasis). a self—form of the verb is used in telugu to express the meaning in sentences (a) and (b) briefly yet clearly.
- **ex**. find out the most appropriate expression from the given choices.
- **he educated his children well/he got his children educated well/he gave his children good education/ he had his children educated.**
- **the famers grew three paddy crops a year/the farmers raised three paddy crops a year/ the farmers harvested three paddy crops a year**
- **they made him give up his fast with a glass of coconut water/ they gave him a glass of coconut water to end his fast/they offered him a glass of coconut water to break his fast.**
- **she built a house in annanagar/she had a house built in annanagar/she got a house built in annanagar.**
- The government arrested the smuggler/ the government had the smuggler arrested/the government got the smuggler arrested
- The children fly kites/ the children make kites fly/ the children have kites to fly/ the children have kites fly.
- The police made him confess his crime/the police had him confess his crime/the police forced him to confess his crime.
- The governor made the minister swear the oath of secrecy/the governor swore the minister the oath of secrecy/ the governor had the minister swear the oath of secrecy.

- The mother helped him do his homework/the mother made him do the homework/the mother had him do the homework.
- The illiterate prisoner had the jailor write a letter for him/ the illiterate prisoner made the jailor write a letter for him/the illiterate prisoner requested the jailor to write a letter for him.

CHAPTER 8

modal auxiliaries

now that **shall** is virtually out of circulation in some major varieties of English, **ought to,** becoming old fashioned, **need** and **dare**, having stopped short of becoming total auxiliaries, there are at present eight modal auxiliaries in english. They are **should, will, would, can, could, may, might** and **must.** modal auxiliaries do not take the infinitive marker **to** and they do not need the operator **do** in negative sentences and questions. u**sed to** needs the operator in negative sentences and questions in some varieties of the language and so it is not a modal auxiliary.

will is used with all persons to express future in formal english. In fact, there are three alternative expressions to express scheduled or definite actions in future. Now the use of **will** is restricted to willingness with the first person or indefinite future with all persons thus:-

i will definitely help you. (It shows the determination of the speaker. w**ill** is a stressed form.) **I'll see him tomorrow. we'll purchase a house after some time. you will regret your hasty decision later. he will do his post graduate studies in the states. i won't see him this week. i won't be seeing him this week**. (all indicate indefinite future. if the actions are scheduled or are expected to take place with some amount of certainty, present continuous is used. thus:—**i am seeing him tomorrow** or i **am going to see him tomorrow.**

if **will** cannot be used in questions with first person, how can **shall** be used with the first or any other person? One cannot ask others about one's future actions or plans. Therefore there is a good case for accommodating **shall** in the company of obsolete words.

should is used to express moral or professional duty or responsibility thus:-**you should help your parents in their old age. you should assist the authorities in discharging their duties**. it is also used for expectations to be shortly or definitely fulfilled. ex. **the train should arrive any moment**. **ought to** is also used in almost the same sense and it can be replaced by **should** at any place. **we ought to help destitute children** is the same as **we should help—.you ought not to speak like that** is the same as **you shouldn't speak like that**. there is a good case for sending **ought to** to the recycle bin as it is somewhat old fashioned, taking, unlike other auxiliaries, an infinitive marker and also because it serves no special purpose.

would is the past tense form of **will** and is used as such in reported speech. ex. he **said," i will do it. "he said he would do it. i said," i'll look into it." i said i would look into it.**

would and used to

would is used to express past habits but **used to** is preferred to it as it is clearer. ex. he **would daily play games with his friends after school hours**. but **he used to play—is clearer**.

would has a strong presence in polite oral discourse for making polite requests, enquiries, and submissions, requiring the indulgence though not the formal permission of others. ex. **would you mind switching off the air conditioner, please? what would you like to have, coffee or tea? i would like to introduce my friend to you** is, however, slightly less formal than **may I introduce—?**

must and should

should is used for obligation ethical or professional while **must** is used for compulsion of circumstances or limitations imposed by an authority private or public in order to avoid penalty, punishment, inconvenience, loss or forfeiting a right. ex. **you must file your income tax returns before 30th July. You must not waste time like this if you want to come up in life**.

You must start now if you want to catch the nine o'clock. as **must** indicates necessity of performing some action, the opposite of **must** is **need not.** As there is no past tense form for **must, had to** is used to indicate compulsion in the past. ex. he **had to clear his debts before the month end to avoid punishment. You need not file income tax returns, if you are a senior citizen and if your annual income does not exceed rs. two hundred thousand.**

can and could

can and **could** are used to indicate ability in the present and the past respectively, ex. he **can speak eight languages fluently now but he could not speak a single word until he was well past three years of age. can** is used for seeking and giving permission for which a person seeking it is not automatically entitled. If seeking or giving permission is a mere formality **may** is used. **could** is used for polite

formal requests or for asking permissions. ex. an **employee to the boss, "can I go home now? I have an emergency call from my sister." the boss, "of course, you can." "can't I go now, please? i have finished my work for the day".**

"**May I come in?**" is a mere formality, used particularly, to draw the attention of someone in an office or class room, entering which without a formal request is not considered good manners. "**culd I have your pen, please?**"

"**could we meet in your office tomorrow, say, at half past ten?**" (Polite requests)

may and might

may expresses possibility or probability. ex. **It may rain in the evening. you may be right. might,** the past tense form of **may,** expresses probability rather than possibility indicating the speaker's unconcern about the veracity of the statement or the result. Ex. he **said it might rain. it might not matter but i am not sure. she might be right for all I know.**

need and dare

need and **dare** are halfway house auxiliaries. they are used as main verbs and also as auxiliaries.

i need money desperately. (i require money—) i **needed money desperately at that time**.(past tense) **I don't need any help from you. do you dare to speak to me like that? He dared to defy his boss**(are you so bold as to speak . . . he was so bold as to defy . . . .).

need and dare are used as auxiliaries in questions and negative statements. Ee. **you need not start now. the train is scheduled to pull out of the station not before ten p.m. need i apologize? how dare you deny the promise you made?** Need and dare are not inflected for person or number and they are normally unchanged in the past tenses. **Need she pay fine for her absence? He need not have paid the penalty**. (The fact is, he paid.)

the auxiliaries in the perfect tense

you should have apologized to her. (the fact is you did not apologize.) he **must not have done** it. (the speaker thinks, based on the nature and circumstances of the case, that he did not do it,) he **need not have committed the blunder**. (there was no necessity for him to commit the blunder but he committed the blunder.)

Exercise 13.

fill in the blanks with modal auxiliary verbs.

- what _____ you do if you are offered the job?
- _____ I use your phone, please?
- the first meeting of our club _____ be held at 6.45 P.M in the lecture hall no.12 on monday, 26 July.
- You _____ come late tomorrow. There isn't any pending work to be attended to.
- I _____ buy sixty meters of this cloth, if you quotation is rs. hundred a meter.
- you _____ submit your application on or before 5th august.

- you _____ not affix postage stamps, if you post it in India.
- i _____ not attend your wedding anniversary. thank you for inviting me, all the same.
- you _____ attend the _____ classes regularly, if you want to secure better grades in tests.
- _____ it be possible for you to attend the function, sir?
- i know he booked the tickets for the show. He _____ have forgotten to bring them.
- how _____ you insult me, an officer, superior to you in rank, aside from being much older than you in age.
- She _____ not have committed suicide for such a simple matter.
- you _____ not have paid attention to her remarks.
- you _____ to bring warm clothes if you are coming to delhi in January.
- you _____ come home before the arrival of your boss or else you have to face the music.
- there _____ be light to heavy showers in the evening' the sky _____ be overcast during the day.
- It _____ not be possible for me. i'm going to be busy all the day tomorrow.
- _____ i answer the question, madam?
- the public _____ have put out the fire before the fire fighting people came to the spot.
- the office _____ be open monday through friday.
- we _____ not give any guaranty. we _____ not refund the amount if anything goes wrong.

CHAPTER 9

tenses

verbs in english have no future tense forms, though there are several ways of expressing future actions, events and situations. verbs are not conjugated for gender. verbs, except the verb **be,** are not conjugated for person or number in most cases. the only relic of the once elaborate system of conjugation which is still extant is the form of the verb in 3rd person singular. English has far fewer inflexions than most other languages. however, English has a complex system of twelve tenses.

All the twelve tenses have been gradually evolved from the main two tenses which are now called **simple present** and **simple past**. The progressive and perfect tenses have evolved through the process of transposition of the present participle and the passive participle. ex. **I have the motor repaired. I have repaired the motor.** Though the two structures convey two different meanings, they originated from the same source. The process which had started with transitive verbs was gradually extended to intransitive verbs as well.

The continuous and perfect tenses are a gain, though we cannot say the same thing about all the perfect continuous tenses. Past perfect continuous and future perfect continuous are rarely used although all the four present tenses are used to express different aspects of the action denoted by the verb. the quintessence of communication is to highlight the information the communicator intends to communicate and to shade the information that the communicator

does not intend to communicate. consider the following sentences, one in the present perfect and the other in the simple past.

i have repaired the watch. (this means the act of repairing is over and you can pay the charges and take it. the speaker does not want to say when he exactly repaired the watch. hence he uses present perfect tense.)

i repaired the watch one week ago. (this means the watch has been lying here for the last one week and it is the customer's mistake not to take it after paying the charges. hence the speaker uses simple past tense.

uses of the tenses

simple present (the verbal phrase consists of only the present tense form of the lexical verb in affirmative statements but the operator **do** is used in addition to the base form of the lexical verb in negative statements and questions. The lexical **be** does not require an operator).

Simple present is used to express, besides abilities, attitudes, characteristics, natural

phenomena and repeated actions, also habits, which, especially, when they are a source of annoyance to the speaker, which are expressed in the present continuous. with the verbs **move, sail** etc it can be used to express actions, which are scheduled to take place shortly, with such adverbials as tomorrow, next week etc. ex. **she swims well**. (she has the ability to swim well.) **she loves her parents. Birds fly. it occasionally rains in winter. he comes to school on time but his sister is always coming to school late these days. they move to their new house any day next week**. the adverbials matching with this tense are **always often, daily** etc.

however, the sports commentators describe the live action, using simple present, because the description is always slower than live action and present continuous becomes inappropriate as it takes more time to utter and as it attempts to give an accurate picture of the scene which is changing faster than the utterance.

ex. **he goes round the wicket and bowls a googly**.

present continuous (the verbal phrase consists of the present tense form of the primary auxiliary verb, **be**, in addition to the active participle of the lexical verb.)

51

present continuous tense is the most commonly used tense. it is used for the actions or events in progress at the moment of speaking or during the recent days, in general, annoyingly repeated actions or occurrences and actions or events already scheduled or planned in not distant future. ex. **they are playing cricket now**. **fast food is becoming popular these days**. **your son is coming to school late these days**. **she is moving to her new house <u>next</u> <u>month</u>**. **our neighbors are going to buy a new car <u>next month</u>**. Adverbials indicating future time have to be used when present continuous is used to express future actions.

present perfect (the Verbal phrase consists of the present tense form of the primary auxiliary verb, **have,** in addition to the passive participle form of the lexical verb.)

present perfect is used to express actions finished at any recent time before the time of speaking, with adverbials like **just now, already** etc. **i have already finished my assignment**. **we have got the office remodeled recently**.

past adverbials do not match this tense. hence sentences like **I have had my breakfast at 9 o' clock** are not well-formed.

perfect continuous (the verbal phrase consists of the present tense form of **have** and the passive participle form of the auxiliary, **be**, in addition to the active participle form of the lexical verb.)

this tense is used to express activities or processes which started sometime before the time of speaking and continue till the time of speaking and may normally continue for some time thereafter. The adverbials indicating the beginning of the activity or the total time for the consummation of it are used to correlate with the tense form. ex. **she has been working for a private concern for the last five years (or since 2004.) i have been waiting here for one hour (or since 9 o' clock.)**

simple past (The verbal phrase consists of only the past tense of the lexical verb in affirmative statements and the past tense form of **do**, in addition to the base form of the lexical verb in negative statements and questions.)

simple past is used to express actions or events which started at some point of time in the past and ended without reference to their duration or their convergence with other events, the points of reference.

i jogged for half an hour yesterday. i met my classmate when I was jogging yesterday at about 7 o' clock in the morning.

past continuous (the verbal phrase consists of the past tense form of the auxiliary verb **be** and the active participle of the lexical verb.)

past continuous is used when the past action was still going on at a particular point of time in the past, considered to be the point of reference. ex. what were you doing at 10 o' clock yesterday? i was watching tv.

past perfect (the verbal phrase consists of the past tense form of the auxiliary verb, **have**, in addition to the passive participle form of the lexical verb.)

past perfect is used to express actions or events which had started before a point time in the past, particularly when the past actions and the actions that had taken place earlier are expressed in the same sentence.ex. **where had you worked before you joined this firm? she said, "i saw the film." she said she had seen the film.**

Past perfect continuous (The verbal phrase consists of the past tense form of the auxiliary verb, **have** and the passive participle form of **be**, in addition to the active participle form of the lexical verb.)

Past perfect tense is used for actions which had ended at any time before the past actions started and past perfect continuous is used if the actions took place continuously until the actions expressed by the verb in the simple past occurred. this tense is particularly useful in the reported speech. ex. **I had been looking after my family business before I joined this firm. I said to her," i have been waiting for one hour." i told her i had been waiting for one hour.**

Simple future (the verbal phrase consists of the modal auxiliary **will** followed by the lexical verb in its base form) simple future is used to express actions or events which will normally take place in future but if more certainty or accuracy is needed in reporting future actions, future continuous is used. **what will you do tomorrow? i will be visiting my uncle's place tomorrow**.

future continuous (the verbal phrase consists of **will** and **be** followed by the active participle form of the lexical verb.)

future continuous is used when we want to describe a future action to be imagined as taking place continuously. ex. **the train will be passing through the tunnel at exactly 6 in the morning.**

future perfect (the verbal phrase consists of **will** and **have** followed by the passive participle form of the lexical verb.)

this tense is used when the future actions or events are imagined to have come to a state of completion at some time in future. ex. t**he train will have pulled out of the central station by 7 o'clock.**

future perfect continuous (the verbal phrase consists of **will have been** followed by the active participle form of the lexical verb.)

future perfect continuous is used, if at all it is used, to describe future actions to be taking place before some other future actions start. **ex. the train will have been passing through the tunnel early in the morning tomorrow by the time we reach the place.**

we can use any other modal auxiliary verb in the place of **will** to express a particular mode to form all the four future structures. **ex. it may rain, it may be raining. It may have rained, it may have been raining.**

tenses and conditional sentences

simple present tense is used in the conditional clauses and simple future or simple present is used in the main clause when we express probable and possible conditions. ex. **If you start now you will be able to finish the work well before sunset.**

simple past tense is used to express highly improbable conditions in the conditional clause and modal auxiliary **would** is used in the main clause to match the tense in the conditional clause. In fact, the simple present can be used to express the hypothetical, improbable or impossible conditions.

ex. if I were the prime minister, I would reform the judicial system. (if I am the prime minister I will reform the judicial system.) if i were a bird, i would fly to mumbai. (if I am a bird I will fly to mumbai.) past perfect is used in the conditional clause and **would have** and the passive participle of the main verb is used in the main clause to match it to express impossible or time-barred actions or events. **if he had worked hard, he would have obtained a first grade in the exam.**

subjunctive mood

subjunctive is rarely used in the present day english, spoken or written. it is not only old fashioned but superfluous we can use normal tense structure to wish something impractical, improbable or impossible. **ex. I wish I did it. I wish I had done it. I wish I could do it.** (Instead we can say **I wish I have done it. I wish I can do lt.**) Instead of you **had better** start now, we can say **it is better for you** to start now.

exercise 14.

fill in the blanks with the correct forms of the verbs, the base forms of which are given in brackets. You may have sometimes more than one correct choice.

- what _____ you _____ if you win the lottery? (buy) (a. what are you going to buy? b. What will you buy?)
- i _____ already _____ youthati can'thelpyouandi'mnot _____tochangemymind.(go)
- little drops of water _____ a great ocean. (make)
- what _____ you _____ with the money i had given you yesterday? (do, do)
- he assured me that he _____=_____ the matter. (examine)
- if he _____ money, he would have cleared his debts. (have)
- At present she _____ in a software company. (work)

- i _____ hereforthelastonehour.(wait)
- now that the cloth store he _____ up in Chennai in 2 001 is successful, he _____ to open a chain of stores in big cities all over the country. (set, intend)
- i need not explain to you why i have done what _____.(do)
- now she lives in Bangalore. two years ago she _____ from chennai. (live)
- now the matter _____ under the active consideration of the government of India.(be)
- they _____ their small car factory to Gujarat after local people _____ violent protests against the establishment of the factory in West Bengal. (shift, organize)
- asolderingiron _____ anelectrician'stoolthat _____ and used for joining wires. (be, be, use)
- areindeerislargedeer that _____ in coldregionsin thenorthernhemisphere.(live)
- we _____ for mysore on monday morning and _____ in the city by one p.m. (leave, arrive)
- it is nice to _____ you.(have, meet)
- she told me she _____ in 1990. (have, get, marry)
- she _____ must _____ mad to divorce him after they were twenty years into marriage. (have, go)
- we _____ you as soon as we _____ the program. (contact, finalize) exercise

identify the tenses in the following short story and comment on the appropriateness of their use in the context.

A heroic deed or a desperate act?

it was a bright sunny morning. After two days of continuous rain, the sun broke through the black clouds in all of its splendor. i had come to see my old parents the day before yesterday. for full two days i had to spend my time in my room, reading books and old magazines, as though I were under house arrest. as i walked to the river bank, little did i know that i was going to witness the most tragic incident in all my life.

The river was in spate. the water was eddying as it flowed down the bridge, carrying uprooted trees. fish, small and big were jumping up and frolicking in the fast current. It was 7 O'clock. the river side was bursting with activity. there were old people who came for their early morning walk. children were playing their favorite games in groups. Birds were chirping from their perches on the treetops. as i was watching and enjoying the scene, I saw a boy of nine or ten running after a cricket ball which, having flown over a heap of bricks, was gliding down the slope. as the ball fell into the river, the boy, in hot pursuit, ran down the steep and slippery slope, and, unable to control his speed, fell in the flood water. he was floating in the current, shrieking for help.

another boy about twelve or thirteen, his elder brother, which i came to know afterwards, quickly ran down the slope, jumped into the river, swam down the river for a moment making a brave but unsuccessful attempt to rescue his brother and save himself. he was also carried away by the current while a group of people in which i was one, who helplessly watched. two days afterwards the villagers came to know that two half— decomposed dead bodies of young boys were found in the paddy fields about a hundred and fifty kilo meters downstream. for several days after i witnessed the tragic incident, there was a nagging doubt in the back of my mind. the younger boy misjudged his speed and slipped into the swirling water. it was a tragic accident. But why did the older boy jump to his certain death? was it a desperate act to save his brother who he loved more than his own life or was he in great fear of facing his parents at home, leaving his brother in the flood water? Most of the so called heroic deeds, in fact, were desperate attempts of week minded people who did what they did out of desperation. There are some mythical and legendary characters who are attributed courageous deeds but they are only myths and legends. Alexander and napolean lived in constant fear of assassination and all their adventures were results of that fear psychosis. hitler committed suicide in a bunker for fear lest he should be prosecuted for genocide and other war crimes. Cowards are known to act in an aggressive way which is mistaken for bravery.

There is a popular legend in andhra pradesh. There was war between two independent principalities for pasture lands that lay between them. The commander of the army, one known for courage, fled from the battle field with his soldiers as he understood that defeat was certain, his army would be routed and all his soldiers would killed or captured alive to be executed after a summary trial. He reached home only to face mockery,

57

ridicule and contempt from his parents and his wife for showing his back in the battle field. Under instruction from his parents or in her own wisdom, his wife ironically asked him to take a refreshing bath as he was tired, fleeing from the battle field. As he entered the bath room, he saw a saari, a pair of bangles and turmeric paste which was used by women as a substance with which they washed and cleaned their body to get a shining golden tint to their skin. Spurred by the insulting treatment from his parents and his wife, the army chief left home, gathered some soldiers, who followed him more out of fear for him than loyalty to him, returned to the battle field and was killed by the advancing army of the enemy.

According to this popular legend, the army chief did a brave act.

But he did what he did as he could not bear the mockery and insulting treatment of his wife and parents. He preferred death to mockery and ridicule at home. Courage is not a part of human nature and on the other hand instinct for survival is. The so called heroic deeds are done either on the spur of the moment as the boy did without a thought about the risk involved or when a person was caught, as it were, between the devil and the deep blue sea, as the foolish action of the army chief illustrates or on account of irrational behavior under alcoholic inebriation or as a result of a kind of mental disorder or paranoia.

CHAPTER 10

prepositions

what distinguishes english from most of the indian languages is its possession of an enormously versatile class of words or word particles, commonly known as prepositions. there were prepositions even when english was inflectional. their increase in number and importance was primarily owing to the readjustments necessitated by a major mutation, namely, the gradual loss of case endings in a maelstrom of bilingual conditions that prevailed after the norman conquest. the human ingenuity, which is, to some extent, common to all life, excels in not merely exploiting effectively all available resources but also turning a loss into a veritable advantage.

prepositions have several advantages over case endings. first, clumsy, at times, unpredictable morphological alterations are to be effected in the noun, the pronoun or the noun phrase which becomes, sometimes, unmanageable as a consequence. prepositions, on the other hand, involve no morphological changes and as a result the nouns can freely function as adjectives and change classes with facility. second, case endings are a totally closed set. prepositions, comparatively, are an open set, accommodating words from other classes and even from other languages. third, case endings are not maneuverable. prepositions are, on the other hand, hugely versatile, producing unlimited phrases, in combination with themselves or with other classes of words.

for example, prepositions reduce the ranks of nouns or noun phrases, converting them to prepositional phrases which function as adverbials, which is one of the most productive features of English. ex. the book is **in the college library.** I met him **at one o' clock.** don't play **with a knife.**

(prepositional phrases, functioning as adverbials, indicting place, time and method.)

the prepositional phrases are used also as qualifiers to complete the noun phrase. the ndian languages, having no qualifiers, have to relegate the head word to the last position of a noun phrase, leading to a certain amount of obscurity. in indian languages we can only say **a parliament member** but in english we can also say **a member of parliament**.

This is possible only because of prepositions. thus, we can see the person or thing denoted by a noun both with or without its attributes. the clumsy phrases like **my one friend**, **their one member** need not be resorted to as the prepositions, combining with pronouns, yield not merely well formed but neatly formed phrases like **one of my friends** or much better **a friend of mine** and **one of them**. Apart from this, the qualifiers are clear and unambiguous.

Compare the following phrases.

- **an english teacher**= a person who teaches english or an english person who teaches a subject
- **a teacher of english** = a person who teaches english.
- **flying planes can be quite dangerous**. (planes that fly or flying of planes)
- **take the water can**.(The can that contains water or the empty can that can be used for carrying water.)

qualifiers, defining or non defining are brief structures for defining or non defining relative clauses. ex. **the boy in a white shirt and blue jeans, at the bus stop, is my second cousin** is a brief structure for **the boy who is n a white shirt and blue jeans**, **standing at the bus stop, is my second cousin**. as qualifiers require a sort of reverse processing they are not common or altogether absent in most of the languages.

prepositional phrases which function as qualifiers are placed immediately after the nouns they qualify whereas the prepositional phrases functioning as adverbials are placed normally at the end of a sentence and can sometimes be moved to other positions as well.

ex. **there are a number of theme parks in chennai. In chennai there are a number of theme parks**. (adverbial phrase)**the theme park near Tambaram is very popular**.(qualifier) If it is placed at any other place, the sentence will be meaningless or its meaning will change. pronouns do not take defining qualifiers as they are already particular.

The boy, in blue jeans, is my cousin (not well formed). **the person, in blue jeans, is my cousin.**(well formed) **they who came first or second in various competitions should sit in the first row.** (not well formed) **those who came**. (well formed)

prepositions combine with most of the common simple verbs to soften, intensify, restrict or expand the basic meanings of the verbs, thus producing a wealth of phrases, which, again, is one of the most productive features of english. As a result of this process we have a choice between a verb like **tolerate** and a verbal phrase like **bear with**. the single word verbs and their two word counterparts are synonymous for all intents and purposes but they convey two distinct shades of meaning. the function of the particle used after the verb **bear** is not that of a preposition proper. It forms part of the phrasal verb, which conveys a deportment of graceful humility for a possible inconvenience for which the speaker expressly does not regret or apologize. the mere wealth of synonyms is not a mark of the resourcefulness of a language. it is the facility that a language empowers its discriminating practitioners to express subtle shades of meaning when employing synonyms in their discourse that is the hallmark of a resourceful language.

prepositions combine with adjectives to form expressions like **at large, by and large**, with adverbs to form **for now, till then, from there etc** with other prepositions to form **by and by, by the by**, with conjunctions to form **because of, except for**, with verbs to form **save for, owing to** etc.

prepositions are combined with simple adverbs such as here, there to form new words such as **therein, herein, thereafter, hereafter.**

besides the simple prepositions, there are an almost unlimited number of complex prepositions like **on behalf of, on account of, instead of, for want of** etc.

sans, versus, per, lieu, par are words borrowed from other languages, which function as prepositions by themselves or combine with prepositions to form prepositional phrases.

words, belonging to other classes like **opposite, near, through, but, save, concerning, regarding** have joined the ranks of prepositions.

using appropriate prepositions

In, at, on, for, by are used to indicate time or place. ex. **in april, in 1990, in the morning, at 7o'clock, on the 15th, monday, on the ground, for two days, by sunday morning. in chennai, in the room, at the bus stop, on the floor, terrace, leave for Delhi, the dilapidated building by the library.**

in, at, by, with are used to indicate manner, method, means etc. **in a slow manner, cruising at sixty miles an hour, at twenty rupees a dozen, cut the branch with a knife, come by car** etc.

prepositions are not used before next, last, this etc. **i went there last Wednesday**. now there is a welcome tendency to omit unnecessary preposition. ex, i **waited an hour** instead of **i waited for an hour**. she is visiting us monday. the omission is very common if **day, week** etc occur in the first position of a sentence as in **friday the children are visiting their uncle.**

a foreign learner of english faces a certain amount of difficulty in choosing appropriate prepositions. for example, should we say, **the shop in the mount road** or on **the mount road**, **at the market** or **in the market, in the circumstances** or **under the circumstances? w**hy should we say **in the middle** but **at the centre?** it may be true that the ultimate proof of learners' proficiency in english is their abilityl in using appropriate articles and prepositions. but common sense and clarity of expression should be the guiding principle and not the usage, which was fixed in circumstances and times other than our own. we write **with** ball pens and **with** pencils now and we don't write **in ink** or **in pencil**. we don't say now **I rang up my wife to congratulate her,** but we say i **called my wife.** usage should change with the changing conditions and circumstances.

prepositions, the simple, common and undistinguished words do not only give a distinct character to english but also continuously provide its users with unlimited wealth of expressions, known for their extraordinary range and reach.

exercise 15.

Identify the prepositions in the short story and comment on their appropriateness of their use in the context.

the monkey and the cobra

it was cricket season in england, the visiting indians were playing a test match against the hosts at lords'. It was playtime forus, school boys, as well. it was a very warm saturday afternoon. We were playing cricket with an improvised ball and a baton the vacant ground, adjacent to a grove of mango trees. suddenly our attention was riveted to a terrible sight. On the branch of the tree near our playing field, a monkey and a full grown cobra were staring at each other. The cobra spread its hood and was ready to strike. At that moment the monkey caught the snake by its neck in a swift move and the next moment they both tumbled down and fell on the ground, the brave monkey still holding the snake's neck as firmly as he could in his grasp. probably the monkey wanted to throw away the dreaded reptile at a distance. but the cobra twisted its entire body, encircled the waist of the monkey with its tail and started squeezing the monkey in its tight grip. we were so stunned by their struggle that we watched breathlessly the terrible drama that was unfolding in front of us. a couple of monkeys from the branch of the nearest tree was also watching the scene. the battle continued for well over ten minutes. we thought the monkey, being young had no chance. he was gradually, it appeared to us, running out of energy. He was getting exhausted minute by-minute. in what appeared to be his desperate thrust, he gathered all his strength and started crushing the neck of the monster. the snake, at last, defeated and dead, became limp in his forearms and released him from its vicious grip. the monkey threw away the carcass of the snake and triumphantly jumped to the branch of the tree where his companions were sitting, grinning gleefully, as we gave a big hand, applauding his efforts.

Could we have appreciated and applauded the brave fight of the cobra, if it had won the battle, giving a mortal kiss to the monkey with its fangs?

Why do the humans discriminate between animals and sympathize one living thing against another? We prayed to god, if god existed, that he should render help to the young monkey to win its battle against a deadly foe or he should make a sudden appearance with or without his concert and crush the cobra's head with his trident or hand wheel and save the unfortunate monkey as god was supposedly famed to have killed a similar reptile, and saved an elephant. Was it because monkeys were closer to the humans than the reptiles on the tree of life? Was it because we generally supported the weaker candidate, the one with fewer chances to win a struggle? Our moral support was normally for the victim of aggression and decidedly not for the aggressor. Was it because the monkeys were harmless to the people and the snakes were dangerous? Was the reptile, the cobra, was a common enemy of the monkeys and the humans? Do we share the biblical belief that satan took the form of a serpent to seduce our mythical innocent mother? If a similar fight were to take place in china, would the Chinese extend their sympathetic support to the monkey or the cobra

exercise 16.

Fill in the blanks with appropriate prepositions/ adverbials.

- i will think _____ a solution after I have looked _____ the papers.
- my close association _____ withmy colleague landed me _____ trouble.
- smoking is injurious _____ health.
- walking is _____ far the best exercise for diabetic people.
- she has been looking _____ her baby sister since her mother fell ill _____ Monday.
- alphonsa mangoes grown _____ maharashtra are superior _____ all other mangoes _____ taste and shelf life.
- researchers have proved that tea is preferable _____ all other beverages.
- thank you _____ subscribing _____ our magazine.
- the matter is _____ the investigation _____ the C B I.

- he was known to be a man of great integrity before he was accused _____ fraud.
- the company will make _____ the damages incurred _____ you during your service.
- the tiger is the native of India but you can see this big wild cat _____ the zoos all _____ the world.
- best dress before he went _____.
- it is like looking _____ for a needle _____ a haystack
- we are committed _____ developing our college _____ a premier institution _____ its kind.
- the car driver was arrested, was charged _____ manslaughter and released _____ bail.
- a mentally retarded person is not responsible _____ his actions.
- my father resigned as D C P as he could not cope _____ the work.
- he insisted _____ doing it himself though I offered my assistance _____ him.

exercise 17.

fill in the blanks with appropriate prepositions/adverbials.

- the recent research shows the human brain developed enormously after the humans have adapted _____ meat eating.
- mysore is famous _____ silks and sandal wood carvings.
- lack _____ science education is the reason _____ indulging _____ superstitious practices.
- the children are more susceptible _____ this disease than adults.
- people who are emotional are prone _____ errors.
- i wish to congratulate you _____ your success.
- people _____ the world rely _____ fish _____ the protein part _____ their diet.
- the brothers fought _____ each other _____ the division of family property.
- a balanced diet is indispensable _____ good health and long life.
- every child has a right _____ education.
- your chances _____ promotion depends _____ yourhard work and efficiency.
- the headmaster served the school _____ thirty years.

- it has been raining ____ yesterday morning.
- the monsoon sets ____ the last week of June.
- deprived ____ nutritious food, the children ____ third world countries develop bloated stomachs.

CHAPTER 11

adverbs

The deictic adverbs of time and place, **now, then**, **today, tomorrow**, **here** and **there**, which define the time and place settings of an event, are a universal set. They are indispensable for clarity and accuracy. The tenses of the verbs can be dispensed with, which will in no way affect the clarity or efficacy of a language. But when the adverbs themselves are ambiguous like **kal** and **parson** in the major segment of the Indian subcontinent, it will impede the processing of the meaning of the expression. The fact that People lived and spoke those languages to conduct their day to day affairs for thousands of years without inventing a device to disambiguate morphologically shows the basic conservative mindset of the people.

languages change in the direction of simplification and the process of simplification is more pronounced in english than in most other modern languages. "The ultimate outcome may be the state of affairs which we see in Chinese where each word is a morpheme and every practical feature that receives expression, it receives it in the shape of a word or phrase". (leonard bloomfield) words and phrases are replacing words obtained through suffixation.**Fast** and **hard** function both as adjectives as well as adverbs and we face no problems in processing their function. we use adjectives where other languages require adverbs as inthe following examples.

it seems/sounds/looks/appears/tastes/smells/feels good. **He takes everything serious.**

object Complement has replaced the adverbial phrase. ex. **we regard/ consider it an asset. (as,** in the kernel construction, **'we regard it as an** asset' is dropped.) **wait an hour for me. (for** is dropped before **an hour.) monday he returns to india.** he **went home.**

(for the reason given for dropping **to** is that **home** is an adverb. **we will meet here next monday. last saturday i visited my grandparents.(on** is always dropped before **last** and **next.** does **monday** become an adverb modified by **next** or **last**? It is not so.

there is a perceptible tendency in progress to drop the prepositions which are not absolutely required for processing the function of a word or phrase. (suffixes/inflections< phrases<single words) as position determines function, the—ly suffix can be dispensed with totally.

ex. **the passage reads good. she sings beautiful. She loves it dear.** They equally make sense as **the passage reads well. she sings beautifully. she loves it dearly.**

the word**, beautiful,** functions as an adjective, placed before or in association with nouns and the same form of the word serves as an adverb, placed at the end of a sentence or in association with a verb as is the case in chinese.

the omission of unnecessary prepositions even in standard variety of english, using short forms instead of the somewhat longish words such as **photo, lab** etc. instead of **photograph, laboratory**, using words without inflections or suffixes wherever possible are some of the processes which are making english simple and user—friendly.

exercise 18.

1. full beautiful, a fairy's child.
2. you are total responsible for your actions.
3. he drove the car careful while negotiating the bridge.
4. i met a friend quite unexpected in Bangalore.
5. they searched continuous for three hours in vain.
6. you have to learn dancing diligent and slow.
7. she donated generous to the orphanages, having no children of her own.
8. your answers are complete wrong.

9. the plants grow nice and beautiful in this soil.
10. they happy married for ten years before they got divorced over a trifle.

Exercise19. expand the adverbs into prepositional phrases.

1. she recorded the conversation faithfully and accurately.
2. he spoke gently and softly while pointing out her errors.
3. he was undoubtedly in the wrong.
4. the destitute was treated kindly and sympathetically.
5. the witnesses were systematically cross-examined.
6. the papers are being closely looked into.
7. the apartments are neatly and cleanly maintained.
8. they have completed the operation successfully.
9. he spoke precisely and to the point.
10. she argued fluently and excellently.

CHAPTER 12

question words and question phrases

kipling had six serving men, **who, what, where, when, how and why,** who are hardly sufficient for our needs. we require at least nine question words and phrases. they are, besides the six, **which, how many/ how much, and howmanieth,** leaving such archaic words as wherefore. there are quite a number question phrases to substitute question words for clarity or accuracy. forming question phrases, particularly in combination with prepositions, is a productive feature.

1. **who**—which person.(Pronoun, common for singular and plural. it has other forms, **whom** and **whose.** Instead of **whom, who** itself is used, particularly, in the spoken variety.) Ex. **Who are they? Who did you see?**
2. **what**—thing, idea, job or profession. (pronoun and adjective) ex. what is it? what is your brother? (pronoun) what sort of books do you read? (adjective forming a noun phrase)
3. **which**—particular thing or person. (pronoun and adjective) It does the same duty as **what. w**hen the choice is open, we use **what** and when the choice is limited to two, three etc we use **which.** ex. what books do you read? which is your favorite beverage, coffee or tea? (as an adjective, it is used for forming noun phrases.)
4. w**hose**—(possessive pronoun, used for persons and living things. ex.**whose coat is this? cuckoo is a bird whose eggs are hatched in the nests of other birds.** for non-living things the phrase **of which** is used. this is the casket the contents of which are missing. this convention need not be followed and we can say. this is the casket whose contents are missing.(as an adjective, it is used to form noun phrases.)

5. w**hy**-for what, or for what purpose or reason can be used instead of **why** to be more specific. (adverb of reason or purpose.) Ex. Why are you irregular to classes?

6. **when**—at what time or what time, in which month or year, on which day can be used for more specific information instead of when.) (adverb of time),

   where—at what place, in which area, on which floor, to which place can be used for more specific information instead of **where.** (Adverb of place),

7. **how**—(adverb or adjective?).—how are you? how is it?

   how—(adverb)—how did you come? how did you do it? (by which means, in which method.)

8. **how** (intensifier)—How many, how much, how often. **how** is used as an intensifier to seek specific information about the number, quantity (to form noun phrases) and combines with adverbs to form adverbial phrases. ex. how many workers are needed to finish the work in time? how much milk do you require? how often do you visit theatres to see films?

9. howmanieth—adjective—there is no question word for the following statement in english but there is one, particularly in south indian languages—rabindranath tagore was the fourteenth child of his parents. howmanieth can be used to frame the question thus: howmanieth child was rabindranath tagore to his parents? he responded to my third letter. to howmanieth letter of yours did he respond?

   most of these question words or phrases are used as relative pronouns as clause markers and as prepositions.

   ex. he is the boy, **who** scored the highest marks in physics.(relative pronoun) I do not know who he is, **what** he does for a living and **where** he lives.(clause markers or subordinating conjunctions. when meeting strangers, we feel a little bit nervous. Use your discretion where, if and when necessary.

CHAPTER 13

discourse markers

discourse markers comprise[1] conversation fillers and [2]transition words. they are complementary to each other, though they function quite differently in a discourse written or spoken. conversation fillers are like speed-breakers to control the rapid movement of speech which may become erratic and unpredictable for want of necessary pauses, turns and directions. but too many conversation fillers may retard the smooth flow of a discourse. the following are some of the conversation fillers. :

well, ok, yes, no, alright, however, nonetheless, nevertheless, by the by, assuredly, sure, absolutely, undoubtedly, coming to the point, true, I mean, you know, I see, you see.etc. the common conjunctions like **and, but** etc also function as discourse markers.

transition words are like road signs guiding the hearer or reader to follow the import and drift of the discourse without a break or impediment. but too many transition words may make the discourse uninteresting and uninspiring. the readers or hearers may take it as an affront if nothing is left to their imagination or judgment. The following are some of the most commonly used transition words:

first, second, to begin with, last, lastly, finally, to conclude, to sum up, on the one hand, on the other hand, on the contrary, to give an example, say, again, to repeat, but. however, nonetheless, nevertheless, now, once, then, this, that etc.

the main difference between the conversation fillers and the transition words is that former give a breather to the hearer to stop and think before proceeding further and the latter lead and guide the reader to follow the design and drift of the discourse to its logical conclusion. the fillers are more frequently used in oral discourses and the transition words, in written ones. there is another kind of fillers, called expletives, such as **damned, bloody**, **hell, shit,** to mention but a few which are used, along with slang, to season conversation with a strong tangy flavor.

Exercise 20.

write the following jumbled sentences in the correct order so as to form a sensible paragraph, using discourse markers as clues.

a.

- to this end it has drawn on the expertise of many scholars throughout the world.
- in the closing years of the 20th century, the English language has become a global resource.
- now english is the possession of every individual and community that in any way uses it, regardless of what any other individual or community may think or feel about the matter.
- The Oxford companion to the English Language seeks to reflect this state of affairs as accurately and as impartially as possible.
- as such it does not owe its existence or the protection of its essence to any one nation or group.
- a list of these contributors and consultants can be found on pages 9 to 14.
- (from introduction to *The Companion to the English language.*)

b.

- at that time it was orbiting at a much greater distance from the sun than it orbits at present.
- once, as mars and Jupiter passed closest to each other in their perihelion orbits, a celestial event of enormous magnitude happened.
- you know that mars is a planet much smaller now than the earth.
- however, one billion years ago, it was about a hundred times as large as our earth.

- it was pulled by the gravitation of the sun on one side and that of jupiter on the other.
- one of these asteroids landed on the earth and brought with it microscopic living organisms which gradually evolved into millions of species on the earth.
- at that critical moment the giant planet, mars, exploded with a bang and was shattered into millions of small and big segments of mass which flew all over the space, the big segments becoming satellites to the planets, including the earth and small ones forming into asteroids. what remained after the big explosion is what is now known as mars, our first home in space and our neighbor now, just a single satellite formed from the debris orbiting round what was once a giant planet.

(based on speculation and not on solid scientific facts.)

c.

1. *finally, amidst the chanting of the sanskrit slokas, the meaning of which nobody, including the celebrant, understands, and amidst loud music, the bridegroom ties the knot.*
2. *on the wedding eve, the bride and the bridegroom, standing at the main entrance of the marriage hall, receive the invitees.*
3. *do you know that Hindu marriage ceremony is an elaborate process during which all those present, including the bride and the groom, may fall asleep in turns?*
4. *in fact, the actual ceremony normally begins in the morning, with the bride and the bridegroom sitting on the stage, tastefully decorated for the purpose.*
5. *once the marriage is over, the invitees are treated to a sumptuous dinner.*
6. *the bride and the groom repeat the vows after the celebrant.*
6. *first, the celebrant asks the bride and the groom to exchange garlands.*
7. *then the celebrant administers marriage vows to the couple.*

d.

- *garnish with coriander leaves and serve hot.*
- *do you know how to make pepper chicken?*

- *first, add chopped onion, green chili, curry leaves, ginger-garlic paste and sauté till they turn golden brown.*
- *add powered pepper and the cooked chicken to this mixture and stir well.*
- *mix well and add water. close the pan with a lid and allow the chicken cook till the water drains.*
  In a separate pan, add oil, mustard seeds, sliced onions and sauté till golden brown and add them to the pan containing the cooked chicken
- *add finely chopped tomatoes and fry till it becomes soft.*
- *heat oil in a pan.*
- *add coriander powder, chili powder clove cinnamon powded and salt to taste.*
  identify discourse markers in the following episode and comment on their appropriateness.

marriage institution in a veritable mess

Judge sathya dev, presiding, the court is hearing the petition of soundarya against her parents mr and mrs ramaswamy, who allegedly intimidated her threatening to commit suicide, if she did not agree to marry an nri dr pratap. prosecution counsel ms. vidya is examining the accused while mrs. vaidehi, the counsel for the defendants is keenly watching the proceedings.

Ms.vidya: [approaching the witness box] as the criminal complaint is against you both, either of you can answer my questions, unless I specifically address one of you, ok? Your daughter is a software engineer, earning rs. 30, 000 a month. so she need not get into a matrimonial mode for her upkeep. bharta, in the vernacular, is one who bears the expenses for supporting his wife. In English, it means tiller of the soil. Either way ms. soundary doesn't need a husband. She has a substantial job and she can support herself with dignity. As you intend getting her married to an nri doctor, you aren't arranging a tiller of the soil for your daughter either and . . .

Mrs kamala ramaswamy: [interrupting the counsel] is it the only reason why people marry, I mean all?

Ms. Vidya: you are answering my questions. I am not in the witness box to answer your questions. all the same I will answer. People marry for sex and . . .

Mrs. Kamala: That is preposterous.

Ms. Vidya: do you mean to say people don't marry for a legal, free and safe sex?

Mr. ramaswamy: what she means to say is that is not the main reason. People want to have their own children to perpetuate their family name, business, if they have any, and mainly to perpetuate their line.

Ms. Vidya: sex is not the primary reason for getting married. Agreed, mr. ramaswamy. People can have safe and not so illegal sex outside marriage with persons of the same gender or opposite gender in a free country like india and it is no crime. Prostitution is illegal in some states, of course. Everything, every human activity, including marriage is commercialized, except sex, in harmony with the prim, smug, snobbish and prudent present day people's accepted social norms and mores.

The judge: are you married, ms. Vidya, by the by?

Ms. Vidya: no, your honor. And my marital status will have no bearing on the present case.

The judge: I will judge whether it has bearing or not. Do you have sex?

Ms. Vidya: what dad? Sorry, your honor.

The judge: will you answer my question?

Ms. Yes, occasionally. If you want further details, I have sex with a boy friend, who is equally unmarried; if you are thinking that I am a spoilsport, disturbing the peace of some other person or family.

The judge: thank you. now you can proceed.

Ms. Vidya: marriage is not necessary for financial security or sex, at least in the present case, to put it bluntly.

Mr. ramaswamy, what about family line?

Ms.vidya: family line, my foot, I'm sorry, your honor, extremely. In our state a number of people share the same family name to whichever caste they belong. To sustain the continuance of your family line, or to put it scientifically, to preserve your own patented copyrighted genes, you unintentionally bring forth more pressure on the hundred and twenty crore sets of genes in the country, on the limited and scarce natural resources. You have no thought, obviously, for your country or humanity at large and all living things, in general.

Ms. Vaidehi: she is insulting my clients, your honor.

Ms. Vidya: if I'm insulting your clients, I'm insulting myself, I'm insulting the entire humankind, for we are all willy-nilly carrying the genes of an idiosyncratic ape which forayed into hazardous situations, compromising its liberty for the sake of marriage and companionship, compromising the safety and security of family to uphold societal norms and so on and so forth. It is agreed now the primary purpose of marriage is neither financial security, nor sex, nor preservation of genes nor perpetuation of a family line.

Mr. ramaswamy: our scriptures say we and our forefathers cannot enter the promised happy worlds unless we have our progeny.

Ms.vidya: not just progeny.you are wrong. you need sons. Do you have a son, mrs. ramaswamy?

Mrs. Ramaswamy: [stifling her tears] we used to have, madam. He is now in the states, living with a foreign woman, having totally abandoned us to fend for ourselves. We expected a huge dowry from our son's marriage, with which we wanted to arrange our daughter, soundarya's marriage. Now we have mortgaged our lands, our house, and we pledged our valuables in order to celebrate, on a grand scale, soundarya's marriage with an nri doctor for which she got us arrested and made us spend a couple of days in police custody.

Ms. Vidya: well, well. Control your emotions, madam. Now you want sons through the line of so called weaker sex as your son has denied that chance. But your scriptures say you need a son and not a daughter to gain a passage to a happy world, I understand. Dasaradh had a daughter through one of his wives, we don't know which one. He badly wanted a son, didn't he? If you really believe in your scriptures, you adopt a son from an orphanage, legally and through chanting of vedic mantras, the exact meaning and purpose of which nobody knows. That solves your spiritual problem. If you have a care for the happiness of your daughter, please stop this kind of blackmail, threatening to commit suicide etc. Besides, I have done some research in this matter. Your nri, your would be son-in law doesn't deserve a marriage. He deserves death by hanging or electric chair. He was already married, having obtained a huge dowry, before he approached you through a marriage broker. He murdered his wife brutally with the help of his widowed mother, having harassed her and her parents for more money. They contrived to make her death appear like an accident though. The cops could not prove a thing against the doctor and his cunning mother.

Ms. Vaidehi: she is inventing a story, your honor.

Mrs. Ramaswamy: we know he was married though we didn't know he killed his wife.

Ms. Vidya: let's get down to brass-tacks now. The case against you is you allegedly bought some poison to take your lives if your daughter refused to marry the nri. Why an nri? Will you enlighten the court, mrs. Kamala.

Mrs. Kamala: my sister's daughter was married to an nri, a software engineer. So . . .

Ms. Vidya: so you damned planned to do better, thus proving yourself better than your sibling, climbing up the ladder of family prestige in the eyes and ears of the society one step ahead of your sister, thus thwarting the cherished goal of your daughter to pursue her chosen career without any let or hindrance from the proposed marriage, thus endangering her life also in the bargain.

Mr. ramaswamy: the society, our kith and kin will look down upon us, if our only daughter is not getting married at the proper time, which was why we resorted to coercion.

Ms. Vidya: kith and kin is a stale phrase, which is nearly out of circulation at present. if one feels one is right, one need not care for society's opinion. Of course, you need a lot of pluck to do that. Therefore you admit you resorted to blackmail and intimidation. the petitioner, your daughter, who got an fir filed against you does not press the charge of attempt to commit suicide. The prosecution case rests, your honor.

Mrs. Vaidehi: well, it is my turn to cross—examine the witnesses. Permit me to examine soundary, the petitioner first, your honor. Please.

[soudarya stands in the witness box vacated by her parents]

The judge: don't ask such silly questions as 'is your name soundarya etc?

Mrs. Vaidehi: ok, your honour. Ms. Soundarya, your parents have done what any parent normally does.

Ms. Vidya: do you mean to say all parents resort to blackmail, coercion and intimidation to force their children into marriage against their will.

Mrs. Vaidehi: The parents did nothing wrong. they wanted their daughter to get married.

Ms.vidya: through blackmail and coercion, my goodness.

Mrs. Vaidehi: please order the learned prosecution counsel not to interrupt me while I am examine the petitioner, your honor. O k ms soundarya your parents did what they did only for your good. You can express your reluctance. Why did you go to the police?

Ms. Soundrya: my parents came to my room with poison bottles. I didn't want to marry, at least now, right at the beginning of my career. i thought they were hell bent on ending their lives. I told them I needed some more time to mull over the proposal, left the room and went to the police station. i Lodged a complaint to save their lives. they are too stubborn to appreciate my view in the matter.

Mrs.vaidehi: your parents had to spend two days in police custody before they were released on bail. Now they stand accused of serious crimes. Haven't you brought disgrace to the family and yourself? How can they show their faces to their neighbours and relations.

Ms. Vidya: let my learned colleague stop moralizing, your honor. There is no disgrace in spending a couple of days in police custody. In fact the petitioner had to bribe the police to file an fir and arrest them in the middle of the night. Nowadays people spend the best part of a year in tihar jail only to be received at home as celebrities with all pomp and jubilation. In fact, the petitioner herself made all arrangements for the release of their parents. Furthermore she is ready to drop all the charges against her parents, of course, if the court permits.

The judge: the parents admitted their guilt. There is no need to waste the time of the court. the institution of marriage like religions were established for the good of the individuals and the society. The institution of marriage, totally crumbling in the western societies, has also suffered cracks in our society with mounting dowry related deaths year after year. Day in day out there are complaints of harassment. Marriage system is in a veritable mess. Arranged marriages without the consent of the offspring are not stable. Don't think I am for love marriages. They are too cinematic to be true. the boys and girls should not enter the matrimonial mode before they attain a mature age of, say, thirty. after that they can seek partners of their choice or remain unmarried to help the country achieve zero population growth. The worst thing is the superstitious belief that the son is the ticket to the other world. There is no other world than this planet, which is suffocated and stifled by over population. Marriage is necessary for the continuance of human race though not the family name unless we adopt an alternative to marriage. The social scientists should explore and find a solution like setting up a gene pool. But the marriage is for companionship also. We should legalize and encourage same sex marriages like they do in of the civilized countries.

the court is pleased to impose a fine of thirty lakhs on mr. and mrs. ramaswamy to be paid to the petitioner in order to enable her to purchase an apartment in the city. The defendants are ordered not to coerce the petitioner into marriage. the petition is thus disposed. and adjourned for lunch. [all rise and the judge leaves the court]

CHAPTER 14

sentence patterns

five distinct elements can be identified in english. they are 1. subject, 2. verbal, 3. complement, 4.object and 5.adverbial or adjunct. south indian languages have only one kind of complement, namely, subject complement. north indian languages, similar to english, have object complement too. english alone across indian languages has what can be called a related Complement because of the presence of a class of verbs, denoting the general meaning of **possess**. the primary verb **have** belongs to this category. the other members of category are **contain, owe, lack, consist of, comprise, possess**, all of which are followed by an element which can be called related complement. as a result of this difference, there are five distinct clause patterns, all of which are derived from one basic pattern, s v c (a).which is a simple equation or identity, s=c (a), v, being a mere connective, is always dropped in south indian languages in order to avoid clumsy constructions with the verb **be** like **he is as an engineer**. In fact, this connective verb 'be' is not needed even in English and hindi. Ex. He an engineer. This boy an excellent footballer.

from the basic s v c (a) pattern, we can derive pattern 2, that is s v a, omitting c, making optional (a) a constituent element. example: **he is a member in the committee =He is on the committee**. If c is not identical to the s but a part of it or in a way related to it we have pattern 3, s v rc (a), which is absent in indian languages. we have sentences like **a monkey has a tail, he owns a house**, **the tumbler contains water**, the meanings of which can be expressed only in s v a pattern in Indian languages. the fourth pattern s v o (a), derived from s v c (**he is the one writing a letter**, rewritten as **he writes a letter**) is common in most of the languages. but pattern 5, s v o c, derived from S V O A, common to hindi also, is absent in south indian languages. **We elected him as**

president, in S V O A pattern is a well-formed sentence and when the preposition **as** is dropped, **a**, a constituent element, gets raised to the rank of c, improving the structure of the sentence somewhat. the 6th pattern, s v o o, derived from s v o (a) is peculiar to english, sounding somewhat illogical. in a sentence, **i gave a book to him**, (s v o a) when **a** is moved to the third position and the preposition is dropped, the **a** is misconstrued as o, resulting in pattern 6. now that **a** is raised to the rank of **o** and renamed as indirect object, it can be raised to the rank of **s** in the passive construction thus-: i **gave a book to him = i gave him a book=He was given a book by me.**

This is an example how patently illegitimate constructions are legitimized by adoption and found acceptance through usage. It also amply demonstrates that grammar has evolved and has not been wired into the brain of a child before its birth.

gerunds and infinitives

a gerund, the—**ing** form of a verb, apart from functioning as a lexical verb in continuous tenses, also functions almost as a noun and hence it is also called a verbal noun. it is an uncountable noun. it functions as a subject, a complement, an object, and an object complement and an adverbial. ex. **walking** is a good exercise for pregnant women and elderly people. (s) strolling gently in the drawing room is not **walking**. (c) i like **walking** in the early mornings. (o) do you call it **walking?** (o c) this place is good for **walking**.

(noun in a prepositional phrase) i saw him walking in the park. (adverbial) gerund is a free element in all these sentences. there are no gerunds in indian languages. in a sentence, i**like him singing gazals**, *(singing is the real object and not him. Hence the sentence is tobe reconstructed as **i like his singing gazals)**

an infinitive, the base form of a verb preceded by **to** as a phrase marker is used as a subject and a complement. **To walk on the railway track could be dangerous. to see** is **to believe (s** and c**).** but when it is used after a lexical verb it gets bonded with the verb to function as a conjoined clause with **to, functioning as a clause marker. a chain of infinitives can be conjoined together one functioning as a matrix to the one that**

follows. the infinitive, if it is transitive or causative, can be converted to passive voice. ex. i would <u>like</u> **to walk.** i tried **to persuade** him **to join** us **to undertake** a trek—they planned **to construct** a number flyovers in the city **to ease** traffic congestion. (active)

a number of flyovers were planned to be constructed for the traffic congestion to be eased in the city.

An infinitive is more like a nuclear clause a clauselet, a halfway house between a noun and an adverbial, between a phrase and a clause. ex. **i wanted to go**. (i wanted that i should go**.) i wanted him to go**. (i wanted that he should go.). **he tried to succeed**. (he tried so that he might succeed.) **i asked him to leave**.(i told him that he should leave. there are Infinitives in indian languages but they are placed before the lexical verbs. the infinitives in the following sentences are used as nouns.

We don't know how to make both ends meet these days. To locate a house in a big city without the correct address is well neigh impossible.

it is used as an adverbial in the following sentences.

to give you an example, a dog does not distinguish colors. To put it in a nutshell, he doesn't deserve the award.

It also functions as an adverb, modifying the adjective, placed after an adjective. ex. **unable to bear the excruciating pain, he committed suicide, i find it hard to believe.**

Participial phrases

Participial phrases are commonly found like infinitives both in inflectional and non—inflectional languages. there are two types of participial phrases in english, the simple participial phrase and perfect participial phrase, both of which can be converted to passive voice. they function as adverbials.

If the subject of the lexical verb is different from the subject of the participial phrase, its subject is placed immediately before it, separated by commas to avoid confusion.

1. **failing to reach the bunches of grapes on the hedge, the fox satisfied itself by concluding that the grapes were sour. having failed to reach—.**
2. **the headmaster, being a strict disciplinarian, the students were mortally afraid of approaching him for favors or for complaints.**
4. **being found unfit on medical grounds, he was not selected for the job.**

the sentence is ill—formed if the subject of the participial does not match the subject of the lexical verb of the independent clause.

- **having been found guilty of a series of murders, the judge sentenced the serial killer to death.** (the subject of the independent clause is **the judge** and that of the participial phrase is **the serial killer**. To make the sentence well—formed, **the serial killer** should be made the subject of the independent clause thus: **Having been found guilty of a series of murders, the serial killer was sentenced to death.**) or **having found the serial killer guilty of murders, the judge sentenced him to death.**

Exercise 21.

identify the elements in the following sentences.

- the physics work-book under review is written by an experienced teacher.
- we will not answer hypothetical questions like this.
- the aero plane was flying over the housetops of the city when it developed a snag in the engine.
- there was once a town in the heart of America where all life seemed to live in harmony with its surroundings.
- then a strange blight crept over the area and everything began to change.
- the feeding stations in the backyards were deserted.

- there are some 5000 languages in use throughout the world of which perhaps may be considered to be of major importance.
- can you name some manifestations of culture?
- his passing away at a youthful age of 49 deprives the world of one of its great artists.
- the government of india awarded him padmabhushan in 1998.
- they called it a day.,
- we consider it one of the worst natural calamities.
- members of the club must pay their annual subscription on before 31st March.
- the police are still investigating the biggest bank heist of the century.
- the kidnappers demanded a hefty ransom for the safe release of the industrialist's daughter.

Identify the sentence patterns in the short story that follows.

A myth

Coercion versus persuasion

Long ago there lived an emperor, whose rule extended to all parts of the indian subcontinent. The emperor, hiran, was ably assisted by shikar, a wise brahmin, in the administration of justice. The emperor was very unhappy because the people were credulous and even idiotic. They wasted their time and the resources which truly belonged to the entire nation in pilgrimages in visits to far off temples and in the celebrations of the imaginary victories and weddings of their imagined deities. Even the poor led their lives in slums but contributed their hard earned money for the construction of palatial structures for gods, whose only real existence was in their deluded mindset. The young people stood in long lines to offer prayers to their fancied gods for their success in their examinations or enterprises. Even when they failed in their efforts they visited temples, all the same, blaming their fate. The emperor, hiran established schools to educate the young people, particularly, to inculcate rational thinking and scientific temper in their minds and in their day—to—day lives. More education made more idiots. an educated idiot is far more idiotic than an uneducated one. More people subjected themselves and their bodies to more absurd and unnatural pain and suffering, like fasting days on end, piercing all parts of their bodies with steel rods and celebrating marriage anniversaries of their gods with pomp and glitz with large hoardings and cut-outs of the images of their gods and goddesses. They used all instruments of communication networks, like literature, art and architecture.

The emperor lost his patience. His advisor was not available for consultation as he was away on some personal business. He could not wait for the arrival of hi advisor. He promulgated ordinances to put an end to the erroneous mindset and repulsive attitudes and behaviour of the people. he ordered that all the temple premises be closed and religious shops be shut down. He got all the people guilty of worshipping their fancied deities flogged publicly and put in prison. His over enthusiastic officers put many innocent people to sword. There was unrest in the country. Shady characters in the government and army used these reforms for settling their personal scores with their opponents. There was witch hunting everywhere because of which even honest and innocent people suffered.

The emperor's detractors spread rumours that the emperor was a rakshas, an enemy of their god, who would take a new avatar at an appropriate time in order to punish him. a canard was also making rounds, floated by the emperor's half brother, that the emperor declared himself e god and ordered people to worship him and only him and none other than him. The emperor, in the opinion of his critics, did not want people to go to the promised happy other world where there would be unending entertainment and enjoyment with no work and no responsibility.

Shukar, the emperor' s loyal advisor rushed to the capital, met the emperor and advised to rescind all ordinances banning religious activities. Hiran, the emperor submitted to his advisor thus:

'sir, you are my preceptor. Is there anything wrong with my views on religion? I am your ardent follower.'

'nothing wrong with your rational opinions, my son. The methods you have chosen to change the superstitious mindset of the people are erroneous. Religions of all sorts have been shaping the mindset of people for thousands of years. You erroneously thought that you could reform the ways of the people in your life time. It takes hundreds of years to enlighten the people. Goutama failed. The charvakas failed. The only way to change the mindset of people is through persuasion, education and good example and not through force, which is counterproductive. You can achieve your intended ambitious objectives only through universal education, corruption—free governance and subtle but sure propaganda to show how rational ideas score over superstitious beliefs. Create a congenial atmosphere for competition of values and ideas. this needs the business acumen of an entrepreneur and not a beneficent dictator.

The emperor realized his mistake, did what his preceptor told him to do and gave up using force to eradicate irrational beliefs in the minds and lives of his people.

One night the emperor had a dream in which he was, in the time machine, to the twenty first century. He found himself in the court of a judge, facing trial for vandalism, violence, with-hunting, persecution and murdering people en mass without trial.

The judge: you have seen the charge sheet. What do you say in your defence? If you need the services of a counsel, the court will provide you one free of cost.

The emperor: thank you, your honour. People believed in gods, devils, astrology, palmistry, immortality of soul and rebirth. I wanted to eradicate superstitious beliefs and i earnestly wanted that the people adopt a rational thinking.

The judge: you don't believe in gods, devils etc. What is god, according to the credulous people?

The emperor: the people believe in a personal god. God is a powerful persona and not a power, which is invisible, impersonal and impervious to flattery or blame one and hence no use to anyone. If god were a persona, he must be visible. What innocent but honest people do is mix god as a persona and god as an invisible power. None, except liars, pranksters, fraudsters or paranoids, has seen him. There is no proof for the existence of a soul or its immortality, avatar god in a human or animal form or rebirth of an individual human being. For one thing, no other religion except Hinduism supports the concept of rebirth. No logic or logistics supports the theory. If all the people are born again and again, we need not one planet but a number of planets to accommodate them.

The judge: i am not a philosopher or one well-versed in metaphysics to enter into an argument r debate with you. I am a judge. You are accused of burning and destroying temples. Many a dictator tried but none succeeded in changing the people's beliefs through force or coercion. Lure of substantial expensive gifts or money made people convert from one religion to another but not from religion to atheism. What is your defence for persecuting people and murdering them for holding on to, in your opinion, erroneous beliefs. Do you plead guilty or not guilty?

The emperor: guilty, no doubt, which is why i rescinded my ordinances and started educating people to give up superstitious beliefs and adopt rational thinking.

The judge: how much have you succeeded?

The emperor : not much, i am afraid. There's first the problem of communication. Language are not capable of clear and unambiguous communication. Words are polysemic. For example, dharma as used by goutama is law, zoological, physical etc. But dharma has at least a dozen meanings, some of which are totally divergent from goutana's meaning. It means 'nature, justice, god of death, charity, duty, tradition, custom, duty enjoined to a person on the basis of caste, the food or money given in charity, alms, propriety etc. Relationships, human or physical are multivalent. The ambient circumstances that actualize an event, physical or psychological are innumerable. we have to reinvent languages before we embark on the task of changing the superstitious mindset of the people.

The Judge: i am holding the court only to conduct an enquiry and not to judge you or sentence you. I leave it to your conscience to judge your actions.

The emperor woke up to find himself in his own bed chamber.

CHAPTER 15

passive voice

most of the Indian languages are null-subject languages as the verbs are inflected for person, number and in the case of Hindi for gender as well. english is almost entirely devoid of inflections except possessive -'s of the nouns and -s inflection of the present tense verb following a subject in the 3rd person singular. so the subject is compulsory in statements and questions. as a result of this, inaccurate, often clumsy and inelegant subjects are used to head the sentences. Consider the following sentences:-

- **one** occasionally makes mistakes in choosing one's/his/her/their life-partner(s).
- **people/they** speak english all over the world.
- **the police** have/has arrested the notorious smuggler.
- **they** make these mobiles in China.
- **the district judge** sentenced the serial killer to life imprisonment.
- **they/someone/somebody** abandoned the new-born baby in the premises of the temple.

normal well—formed sentences without expressing the subject are possible in inflectional languages but not in english. passive voice has gained importance, particularly, to avoid awkward subjects. by using passive constructions, we can reframe the above sentences thus:-

- **mistakes are occasionally made in choosing life partners.**
- **english is spoken all over the world.**
- **the notorious smuggler has been arrested.**

- **these mobiles are made in china.**
- **the serial killer was sentenced to life imprisonment.**
- **the new-born baby was abandoned in the premises of the temple**.

there is a tendency to use passive voice when there is a clear performer as subject. for example:-1.**our grandmother, who passed away last week, used to tell us interesting stories. 2. call the fire service people. 3. Take rest for a week. 4. the prime minister will visit america next week.**

if the above sentences are changed into passive voice, the import of the communication is badly affected or totally lost. passive voice is frequently used in scientific reports for the sake of objectivity. but too many passive constructions will make any writing including scientific writing monotonous and even uninteresting.

normally, the agent following the prepositions by, **with** or **at** is omitted as it is unimportant, redundant or already implied in the verbal phrase or in the context. sometimes the agent is mentioned, particularly, when the end focus is required to be placed on the agent of the action thus: **No, This report was not written <u>by me or any one of my</u> colleagues. I will prove it.**

the sentence patterns s v a (a) and s v c(a) have no objects as elements so they have no passive structures. If s v o is transformed into passive, we will have s v (a)

the following table shows how to change active voice into passive voice. the lexical verb is always in the passive participle form of the verb in the passive construction. hence **bitten** is used in the passive structures as the lexical verb is **bite** in the examples that follow. The additional auxiliary verb, used in the passive constructions is **be** and it is used in the same tense form as the lexical verb in the active constructions.

tense	active	passive
simple present	a dog bites a man.	a man is bitten by a dog.

(the additional auxiliary verb **be** is In the present tense form, **is**.)

continuous	a dog is biting a man.	a man is being bitten by a dog.

(the additional auxiliary verb **be** is in the active participle form, **being.**)

perfect	a dog has bitten a man.	a man has been bitten by a dog.

(the additional auxiliary verb be is in the passive participle form, **been.**)

perfect continuous	a dog has been biting a man.	a man has been being bitten by a dog.*

simple past	a dog bit a man.	a man was bitten by a dog.

(the additional Auxiliary verb **be is** in the past tense form, **was**.)

continuous	a dog was biting a man.	a man was being bitten by a dog.

(the additional auxiliary verb **be** is in the active participle form, **being**)

perfect	a dog had bitten a man.	a man had been bitten by a dog.

(the additional auxiliary verb **be** is in the passive participle form, **been**)

perfect continuous	a dog had been biting a man.	a man had been being bitten by a dog.*

simple future	a dog will bite a man.	a man will be bitten by a dog.

(**the additional auxiliary verb be** is the base form, **be.**)

continuous	a dog will be biting a man.	a man will be being bitten by a dog.*

(the additional auxiliary verb **be** is in the active participle form, **being.**)

perfect	a dog will have bitten a man.	a man will have been bitten by a dog.

(the additional auxiliary verb be is in the passive form, been.)

perfect continuous	a dog will have been biting a man.	a man will have been being bitten by a dog *
infinitive	they have to finish the work,	the work has to be finished by them.
imperative	open the window.	let the window be opened.
	let him do the work.	let the work be done by him.
causative	we made him apologize to her.	he was made to apologize to her.

- **they are not normally used in either spoken or written english.**

if we transform s v o o sentences into passive, we get s v o (a) or s v a (a) ex i gave him a present. (active) he was given a present by me. (passive 1) a present was given to him by me. (Passive 2)

s v o c= s v c (a) ex. they made him captain. (active) he was made captain. (passive)

some verbs take **with** or **at** instead of **by.** ex. **your attitude to work pleases me—i am pleased with your attitude to work—his impudence astonishes me—i am astonished at his impudence.**

Semi-passive is preferred when there is no specific doer or when the recipient of the action is also a doer or is partly responsible for the occurrence. Consider the following sentences:-

he got injured in a traffic accident. he got married twice and he got divorced twice.(semi-passive) **he was injured in a traffic accident. he was married twice and he was divorced twice.**(passive) **exercise 18.**

transform the following sentences into passive voice, adding the agent wherever necessary.

- the prosecution did not prove him guilty of the crime.
- They have elected him secretary for a second term.
- The authorities are looking into the matter.
- the scientists discovered a new galaxy.
- we should purify ground water before using it as drinking water.
- i did not know that he was wanted by the police.
- you need not file income tax returns if your annual income does not exceed Rs. One hundred and fifty thousand.
- they are investigating the daring bank heist that stunned the public.
- they will dispatch the passport to you within a fortnight.
- the academy gave the playback singer a prestigious award.
- you have to treat the differently—abled people with sympathy
- more people speak hindi than any other language in india.
- the police have arrested the notorious smuggler.
- you cannot do it alone.
- four masked men kidnapped the seventeen year old school girl in a white ambassador car.

CHAPTER16

types of clause

three types of clause can be identified in english. they are independent, semi-independent, dependent and reference clauses. if a clause does not contain a main verb and yet makes complete sense it is called a reference clause. exclamatory words or phrases, short answers and question tags which mainly occur in oral discourse are reference clauses. ex. **Is** he an engineer? (**is** is a lexical verb) Yes, he is. (**is** is an auxiliary verb, substituting **is**) He **saw** you, **did**n't he?(**saw** is a lexical verb and **did** is an auxiliary verb)

a sentence may have one or more clauses, depending on whether it has one or more lexical verbs. a dependent clause functions as an element (**s, c, o** or **a**) of the independent clause and it is governed by a clause marker expressed or implied. if a clause is not a constituent of another clause and if it is not governed by a clause marker expressed or implied it is an independent clause. it is the independent clause which determines whether the sentence is a statement, question or imperative.

linkers such as **and, but, or, not only—but also, either—or neither—nor** join similar clauses and hence they are not clause markers. example:-

i don't know <u>and</u> i don't want to know what he is <u>and</u> where he is working.

the first **and** is joining two independent clauses and the second one is joining two dependent clauses. the conjunctions like **that, though, if, whether** etc are clause markers.

the clauses that are headed or governed by the conjunctions are dependent clauses.

However, semi-independent clauses, though headed by clause markers like dependent clauses, are different in their structure, place and function from dependent clauses.

ex.1. **He is not a successful civil servant, for he is honest and upright**. (it is not an adverbial clause because its position is fixed. It is not an independent clause as it is headed by a clause marker **for. Ordering of clauses is also reverse i.e from result to reason, requiring reverse processing, a normal feature of dependent clauses.**

Ex.2. **hitler always suffered from a sense of inferiority and insecurity, which made him aggressive.** (there is no antecedent for the relative pronoun **which.** It qualifies the entire independent clause (hitler's suffering from a sense etc.) and not a particular noun in the independent clause. the pause that separates the two clauses in both examples is longer than the one that separates the dependent structure from the independent structure as the comma indicates.) these examples show that we cannot easily pigeonhole structures, for things or ideas are in a continuum and not in easily separable compartments.

Dependent clauses are of four kinds, 1.noun clauses, 2.relative clauses. 3.adverb clauses and 4.conjoined clauses or intensifier clauses.

1. **noun clauses** or **constituent clauses**. a noun clause functions as the subject, the object, or the complement of an independent clause. like a noun it can also be governed by a preposition in the independent clause. the clause marker of the noun clause is **that**, which is more often implied than expressed. it is always dropped before wh—words which function also as conjunctions. examples:-

what he says is not true. **what constitutes a permissible evidence** is what an accused admits in the presence of a magistrate. I don't know **(that) he is an engineer**. I am not aware of **what he wrote to you**.

2. Relative clauses, _(adjective clauses or embedded clauses) function as qualifiers of nouns. modifiers are commonly used instead of

relative clauses in south indian languages. the relative pronouns, used immediately after the nouns they qualify, function as clause markers. the relative pronouns are **that, who, whose, which. Where, when, how** also function as relative pronouns. only non-defining clauses are embedded after personal pronouns as personal pronouns themselves refer to particular persons or things. **He**, in the sense of any person, is an exception. examples:-

this is the film **which won an academy award.** this is the photo **I spoke of**.

the criminal **who was arrested yesterday** managed to escape. i know the place **where it is available in plenty**.

relative clauses are defining or non-defining as they define or identify the antecedent after which they are placed or they give additional information about them, having already been identified. ex. **the civil supplies commissioner who was caught taking a bribe was suspended.**(defining) **our area civil supplies commissioner, who was caught taking a bribe, was suspended.** (non-defining)

3. conjoined clauses. A pair of conjunctions like **so—as, so—that, such—as, such—that, more—than** join the dependent clause to the independent clause, the first conjunction in the independent clause functioning as an intensifier. examples:-

it proved to be more useful than I thought at first.

it is not so easy as you think.

the problem is so complicated that one cannot easily solve it.

4. adverb clauses or adjoined clauses. as most adverbs, adverbial clauses have no fixed position, though they usually occur after the independent clause, giving the place, the time, the reason and the condition for the status or action, denoted by the verb in the independent clause. the clause markers of the adverbial clauses are **when, where, because, though. If, until, unless** etc.

he got married when he was thirty. when he was thirty he got married.

he could not attend the function because he was quite unwell. because he was quite unwell, he could not attend the function.

reference clauses:—exclamatory words or phrases, short answers, question tags are reference clauses. they occur in oral discourses. short answers and question tags are needlessly stylized. Examples:-

- **Is he an architect**?—yes.(the answers yes, no, of course, sure, ok, undoubtedly etc are good enough and the stylized answer **yes, he is** is needless.
- you have done the work, **isn't it?** Isn't **it, is it, considered by** sticklers as indian english are good enough. In all Indian languages such question tags are commonly used. stylized question tags like **haven't you?** are needless, requiring unnecessary grammatical operations.

Exercise 22.

identify the clauses in the following passage.

Another myth.

A battle for gold

Long ago there was a wealthy farmer who was well known for his honesty and loyalty to the king of the land. one fine morning he yoked the best oxen to the plow and went to the field.

he had many servants but he took pleasure in plowing the field himself. as he was plowing the field, he found a silver casket in one of the furrows. when he opened the casket, he saw a good number of slabs of gold. as he was an honest man, he sent message to the king about his find, for he was entitled only to the produce from the farm land and not to the precious treasures that were found in its bowels. the king of the land sent his eldest son, the crown prince, with his younger brother to fetch the gold to the capital city for he could not trust his servants with so much of the precious metal. The princes collected the treasure trove, put it on their chariot and set off at a great pace to return home. as the princes were tired and as the winter night fell suddenly, they found a vacant cottage on their way and slept there till daybreak.

As the princes were about to set out on their journey home in the morning they spotted a golden buck frolicking and grazing in the grass field. the crown prince asked his younger brother to stay at the cottage to take care of the treasure and started his hunt on foot to catch the strange animal. of course, his younger brother, in actual fact, his step brother, warned him against the fruitlessness of the hunt. However, he respected and feared his elder brother so much so that he could not violate his order and stayed in the cottage and waited for the arrival of his brother. his brother did not return even till midday and even till evening.

as the sun was about to set, the younger brother became restless. he could not wait any longer. he dreaded facing the wrath of his father if he returned home without his brother. his elder brother was the apple of his father's eye. as he left the cottage in search of his brother and walked a little distance he saw his brother returning without the golden buck. he told his younger brother that it was not a golden buck after all but an animal merely painted gold. as they returned to the cottage, they saw a man in royal dress sitting on the driver's seat of their chariot ready to whip the horses. he said to the princes so loudly that they could hear him, 'beauty and wealth belong to the clever and the brave. you are like the greedy hunter who lost the bird in his hand to catch two in the bush. in fact, this treasure trove once belonged to our city. it is ours now again.' so saying, he set off on the chariot at a great speed. now the brothers understood that the golden buck was a ploy of their enemy king, whose capital city was on an island in the godavari river, where the river branched off into two streams before joining the sea. the princes did not want to go home without the casket of gold. They befriended a tribal chief who was living in a thick forest, having been exiled by his elder brother, the ruling chieftain.

The crown prince, concealing himself behind a tree, shot the chieftain with a powerful arrow. when the dying tribal chieftain asked him why he wanted to kill him, the prince said that he cohabitted with the wife of his younger brother and the punishment in his country for such a crime was death. his younger brother's wife was like his daughter, he said. When the chieftain further asked the prince why he had shot him with an arrow, hiding himself behind a tree, instead of facing him in a battle, the prince said that the tribal people were like wild animals of the forest and they could be hunted and killed the way he had shot him.

As the chieftain died his younger brother was crowned chieftain on his promising to the princes that he and his army would join them in their battle against the island king, who had stolen their treasure trove. Of course, the chieftain himself committed a worse crime by cohatting with his elder brother's wife, who was like his mother. But he was his friend and one should search for virtues and not vices in one's friend. justice and morality were double edged weapons in those days as they are now. We hunt with the hound and run with the hare every moment of our life, don't we?

Thus the princes gathered an army of sorts, built a makeshift bridge across the river godavari and laid siege to the island city. a battle raged for several days. finally the crown prince killed the island king in a duel with the help of the king's younger brother. the army searched the city for the casket, found it in a secret place in the royal garden and handed it over to the crown prince, who, desiring to test its purity, ordered his younger brother to place it in the big fire made for the purpose. as the prince saw the gold slabs melt in the fire, he ordered his brother to put out the fire and place the pure metal in the casket after it cooled. then the princes thanked the chieftain for his help, crowned the island king's younger brother king of the island city, made the once independent state their vassal and set off on their chariot to their native city.

The crown prince got himself crowned king after the death of his father. During his just rule he showed his true valour in administering true justice, an example of which was cutting off the head of an unarmed sudra who was doing penances in violation of manudharma. The people believed that not only a brahmin child was brought back to life by the noble king's brave act (in actual fact no brahmin child, as tha people believed, was brought back to life) but the sanctity of heaven was protected as a sudra was rightly prevented from sullying heaven with his ignoble presence by doing illegitimate penances.

The king became old. One night he had a dream in which he found himself being transported in the time machine to the twenty first century. He was being prosecuted in the court of a judge in a small town, gudiwada, in a.p, india.

The judge: you always treated women disdainfully and even inhumanly. Killing them and assaulting them was a sport for you. Why did you kill, unprovoked, the unarmed tribal woman on your way to fetch the box of gold from the farmer?

The king: 'According to our customs, the king had the power over the life and property of his subjects. Apart from this, the tribal woman abused and challenged us as we were crossing her field of ripe maze. I was provoked by her arrogance and impetuosity and I shot her dead. When one of her sons came to attack us, I killed him as well.'

The judge: you were yourselves guilty of trespass and when she rightly challenged you, you killed her and her son. You are guilty of murder, according to your own confession. Second, when a young tribal woman approached you and your brother with the intention of courting you, marrying you or for having a short affair with you, you should have politely declined her hand and treated her with tolerance and understanding. Instead you instructed your brother to cut off her nose and ears. This was an assault on a helpless woman's body, dignity and self respect.

The king: That night as we were taking rest in the abandoned cottage after a long and arduous journey, the woman disturbed us, mocked at us, called us a couple of imbeciles and homosexuals and tried to attack us when we rejected her proposal.

The judge: when her tribal men came to attack you, you shot them all dead along with all their women and children. Aren't you guilty of genocide as well as murder?

The king: Are you holding a kangaroo court, pronouncing judgment without a fair trial? If I had not killed them, they would have killed us. When I killed the tribal woman or her son or the army of tribal men, I did it in self defence.

The judge: even children and babes in mothers' arms? What could have they done?

(the king remained silent)

The judge: and then, you killed the tribal chieftain, concealing yourself behind a tree and when the dying man questioned you, you told him that tribal people were like animals which could be hunted in the like manner. Why did you kill him in the first place?

The king: to honour a pledge given to a friend.

The judge: o.k. Why did you shoot him, hiding behind a tree? Was it because he was an animal? If he had been an animal why did you accuse him of violating an ethical principle sacrosanct only in urban and civilized societies and not among animals? Is this not adoublethink and a doublespeak?

The king: doublethink and doublespeak are not cognizable offenses even according to your own criminal code. Anyhow, if I had challenged him for a duel, he would have the choice of place, time and weapon. I knew that he was far superior to me in strength and handling of all kinds of known weapons. There is nothing unfair in battles, at least in our times. Winning was all that mattered.

The judge: you should have told him the same thing frankly.

(the king remained silent.)

The judge: toward the end of your reign, you performed *aswamedha yaaga*, challenging the people in the country to submit to your sovernity and supremacy or fight with you and get killed. How many people did you kill and how many cities did you destroy to show your eminence?

The king: i subjugated many independent kingdoms, killing thousands people to perform *aswamedha yaga* as prescribed in the *dharma sasthras* to establish my supremacy and serve my people. My ministers and my advisers praised me for my achievements.

The judge: of course. one hare-brained director in recent time made a film based on your so called merit orious achievements. you lived your entire life perpetrating senseless violent acts. You were born in the land of the Buddha. This country always considered *ahimsa* as the highest law. Besides, all your actions are indefensible. What you offered in your defence is wanting in internal consistency. when you are not an ideal person, how can you be considered an ideal king? An ideal king does not exercise power over the life and the property of his subjects. He acts like a true trustee, living and even dying for protecting the life and property of each and every one of his subjects. Finally, you are guilty of murder. You killed an innocent unarmed sudra. This murder has all the attendant characteristics, reasons and circumstances of a cold-blooded murder. This was not done in self defence. This was an intentional act and a premeditated murder. Of course, the sudra was an idiot, who believed in the immortality of soul, swarag and god. He aped the upper caste people who wasted their time and resources like burning precious fat to appease non-existing deities, not in their wisdom but in total foolishness. What explanation can you give in support of your action?

The king: according to the treatise authored by manu and our customs, a sudrs was prohibited from doing penances, for which reason I had to cut off his head, a punishment prescribed by manu for such illegitimate acts. According to our sasthras, a sudra should be prevented from entering heaven by all means.

The judge: rubbish and nonsense. According to our constitution, you are guilty of genocide and murder. Besides, an ideal person is expected to abjure actions which are considered wrong deeds in any community or society and at any time or in any clime. However, I am not holding this trial in this court to pass any sentence on your life and conduct. I leave it to your conscience to judge your actions. The court is adjourned.

The king woke up, shuddering. He was happy and fortunate to live among credulous masses [with the sole exception of jabali and his charvaka crowd, of course], who not only considered his administration of justice to be just, ideal and perfect but also considered him a god man.

CHAPTER 17

reported speech

reported speech is used to make a succinct, brief and clear report of a conversation, a speech or a debate. this is particularly useful in writing minutes of meetings. as different procedures are adopted for reporting different kinds of sentence, we will start with the types of message. When one wants to give information, one uses a statement format in which **subject** precedes **verbal.** the structure remains unchanged when reporting statements. as reporting verb is normally in the past tense, present tenses are changed to their respective past tenses and the statements, functioning as noun clauses are integrated into the main clause with the conjunction **that** expressed or implied thus:-

the chairperson <u>says</u>," i welcome everybody to today's meeting."

the chairperson says (that) he/ she welcomes everybody to the meeting.

the chairperson said, "i welcome all the members to today's meeting."

the chairperson said he/she welcomed all the members to that day's meeting. or better still]

the chairperson welcomed all the members to the meeting held that day.

to seek information from others we frame questions of type (a)or (b), open choice questions headed by question words and the closed choice questions headed by auxiliary verbs. as question words or phrases function as conjunctions as well, the type (a) questions are integrated with the reporting clause which functions as the independent clause. as the independent clause determines the type of the sentence and as the reporting verb shows it is a statement, a request or an enquiry, the noun clause is always in the statement form thus:-

i said to him," what do you do for a living?" i asked him what he did for a living.

did you ask her," why do you prefer engineering to medicine?" did you ask her why she preferred engineering to medicine?

as type (b) questions are not headed by a question word, as the answers are limited only to two options the conjunction **whether** is used to integrate the noun clause with the independent clause thus:-

"do you wish to relax or join me for a walk?" i asked her. i asked her whether she wished to relax or join me for a walk.

imperative sentences are added as infinitives to the reporting verbs such as **request(ed), order(ed) advise (d)** etc. an appropriate reporting verb has to be chosen as the imperative is used to convey messages ranging from a very polite request to an inviolate command thus:-

he said to the mob," please be patient." he requested the mob to be patient.(request) she said to the patient," don't exert yourself." she advised the patient not to exert himself/herself.

the teacher said to the students," be regular and punctual in attending classes." the teacher told (instructed or advised) the students to be regular and punctual in attending classes. (or) the teacher told the students that they should be regular and punctual in attending classes.

the officer said to his subordinates, 'stand in a line.' The officer ordered his subordinates to stand in a line.

'what I advise you is, "Work hard,"' he said to the cadets. He told the cadets what he advised the cadets was work hard. (the imperative is retained after **is** or **was**).

a request or command can be expressed through a question, in which case it is treated as an imperative and added to the reporting verb as an infinitive thus:-

the boss said to miss mary," will you please type the letter and bring it to my room. it is very urgent." the boss told (or instructed) miss mary to type the letter and bring it to his room as it was very urgent

"could you please open the lift door," said the old lady to a young man standing near the lift. the old lady urged the young man standing near the lift to open the lift door. "let's go to the canteen and have tea," said rakesh to his colleague. rakesh proposed to his colleague that they go to canteen and have tea.

the exclamatory sentences are only affirmative statements uttered in an emotional way so they should be restructured as statements and integrated into the main clause with the conjunction **that** expressed or implied thus:-

"how nice of you to be here with us on this occasion, dear madam," said george to mrs. margaret, welcoming her to his shopping mall. george, welcoming mrs. margaret to his shopping mall, told her that it was very nice of her to be there with them on that occasion.

exercise 23.

change the following into reported speech.

- "what can i do for you?" the receptionist said to him.
- he said to her," we will meet in the hotel lobby." "which hotel do you mean?" she asked him. "you mean the hotel i'm staying in or the one in which you are put up?"
- "will you, please, wait for me? i'll say bye to my mum and join you in a moment," she said.
- "don't get confused with red herrings but get down to brass tacks," she said to him.
- "what a pleasure to meet you again!" said he to his friend on the lawns of a star hotel. "the pleasure is equally mine. we haven't met in eons after our college days." said rajesh.

- "those who have booked on thai air lines flight NO 45 are requested to report at counter NO 2 one hour before take-off time. thank you," said the announcer.
- "you look stunning in this dress," he said to his wife appreciatively. "you are kidding, aren't you? no one praises his wife like that, particularly, when they are five years into their marriage," said mrs. raghu.
- "have you seen the latest flick of the mega star, dhanunjay?" he asked his friend.
- the doctor said to her," don't worry. nothing serious. take complete rest. by the by, how is your son, mrs. mala?" "he is fine, doctor, thanks to you. are you prescribing any diet for me?" said mala. "no, you can eat anything you like provided you don't eat too much," said the doctor.
- "will you, please tell me how to get to the nearest police station? i have to lodge a complaint. my pocket was picked while I was travelling in the bus." prakash asked a passer-by. "it is very near. walk straight. turn left opposite that red building. walk to the end of the street and turn right. the third building to your right is the police station." said the passer-by. "thank you so much," said prakash as he proceeded to his destination.

exercise 24.

report the following exchanges between a psychiatrist and his patient.

p: may I come in, doctor?

s: Yes, enter. will you please lie down on the couch?

p: thank you. I don't know how to begin——.

s: well, take your own time, young man. first relax. you are in safe hands.

p: i hope so. since I attended my friend's funeral, I have a feeling that I'm dead myself, doctor.

s: you are what?

p: i mean i am no more. i'm dead. i am a ghost.

s: but it's absurd. you see. You are able to talk to me. I'm able to see you, lying on the couch. you aren't dead. I'm sure you are as alive as I or anybody else, for that matter.

p: your words, however soothing they be, doctor, cannot change my belief. i've been told you are the best shrink in this town. i don't believe in oral assurances, sir. I believe in scientific experiments. i am a sciensist. conduct an experiment and prove i am not dead. i will pay you twice your normal fee and i will be grateful to you all my life, please, doctor.

s: o.k. no problem. living people alone breathe. but i don't have the necessary apparatus to prove you are breathing. i've another idea though. i'll conduct a very simple experiment. only living people bleed. do you, or don't you agree?

p: yes, absolutely. no doubt about it. i do agree.

s: i have a syringe here. i'll extract a few drops of blood from your, say, right hand. fold your shirt sleeve a bit. yes, that's good. you see this is an empty syringe. there won't be much pain. (conducting the venipuncture) now i release the blood, i mean your blood, on this cotton ball. there is blood. you see. what more proof do you need to prove you are alive and not dead?

p: (rising from the couch) excellent, doctor! no more proof is necessary. i think you are a genius. you've demonstrated that dead people also bleed!

Exercise 25.

change the direct speech passages to reported speech and the reported speech passages to direct speech and rewrite the discourse.

The human condition

I saw, in my dream, a man, as though carrying a heavy burden on his back, walking unsteadily in a pathless desert or in a desert crisscrossed by many invisible pathways. his back was bent. he was not old, yet his legs were tottering and doddering. he met an old man or at least, he looked so, with a shaven head and a cleanly shaven beard. he was a buddha [a pure intellect]. the buddha asked him who he was, where he was going and what he was carrying on his back. 'i am an Indian' he replied, 'i am going to a place where I am expected to get relief from my travails and burdens.' The buddha told him he could not see anything on his back and his burden was only a figment of his imagination. 'no, sir, i have a feeling that some people are sitting on my back. i sure hear their voices.' the buddha said, 'true, but those who are piggyback, firmly seated on your back as you imagine are not real people. they are mere ghosts. they are the ghosts of all the nations and of all the past ages. being an indian you are harassed by imaginary things like gods, god men and ghosts. for instance, there are no marxists, leninists or maoists in the land of marx, lenin or mao. but you have their ghosts in india. you are in the land of ghosts and godmen. if the indian maoists want to end exploitation of the poor by the rich, the best way is to kill all the defenseless poor people, living in the villages and the tribal people living on the hills and in the dense forests, which is easier than killing a well protected landlord here or a fully armed police officer there. the goal is achieved. They are not anyhow bothered about the means. Actually the best way to end poverty, in my opinion, is in the hands of the poor people themselves. they have to adopt the policy of one child fora couple or much better no child as long as a couple is poor or no marriage until a person is sure that he/she will be able to ensure healthy living and decent education to his or her offspring without seeking free tv sets or free rice from the populist governments and politicians, who want people to love their wretchedness and loll in poverty, regarding their penury a blessing. they are given free food, shelter and entertainment, though they are not given jobs to live in dignity.

they are then expected to populate the slums and ensure vote banks to their masters. China has shown us the way in this matter. Those who head our governments, it is sad, lack foresight and statesmanship. Instead of taking stringent measures to control population growth, they want to dot the land with atomic reactors and thermal power plants which may prove disastrous in times of tsunamis and earthquakes. your rulers have no proper understanding of priorities.' 'do you mean to say that the poor and the rich divide in this country need not prick my conscience? If we intend to end poverty, the principle of **One and only one child per**

couple should be adopted universally, voluntarily or it should be made compulsory if necessary. but what about securing a place in the promised happy other world. can I worship these god men?' he asked the buddha. 'there is no life after death and you go nowhere after death. Charvakas long ago dismissed the notions about the immortality of soul, the existence of god, heaven and hell.

Bhasmeebhootasya dehasya punaraagamanam kutah
Tatrapridhivyadeeni chatvari tatvani tebyaeva dehakaara
Parinaitanyam kinvadibhyo madasaktivat chaitanyam upajayate
Teshu vinashteshu satsu svayam vinasyati
Nasvargo naapavargova naivatma paraloukikah.

all of the god men are scoundrels who set up their cheating shops, requiring no investment, in order to fleece the gullible people. i do not blame these cheats. i blame the governments which impose rules, restrictions and permit systems for starting any business but close their eyes when it comes to this god man business. some politicians, judges and police officers, in order to have a share in the unearned ill-gotten loot, are cohorts, abetting the heinous crimes of these swindlers, who use magic and sleight of hand tricks to deceive people. this is a billion dollar illegal and immoral business in india.' 'but what about worshipping in the holy places like temples, churches, mosques and gurudwaras to obtain the grace of god?' he asked.'now this is a trillion dollar business in india. we have many religions which are harassing the people, acting as deadweight to stall the liberation and progress of people. christ, mohammed and goutama were rebels and liberators of their people. christ used parables to drive home his points. if he had said that he was the son of god, I don't think he actually said so, he meant that we were all children of god and were all equal in the use and enjoyment of natural resources. he was against worship of god in public places. mohammed also said the same thing. christ was not executed by hebrews or roman rulers but by his followers who took his words too literally and subverted his message. mohammed practiced monogamy but diluted his message somewhat to assuage his libidinous male chauvinist followers and asked them to restrict their harem to four members.

His sensual, lustful followers misinterpreted his message and held the notion that he permitted polygamy. first he said that one could worship god in any place but later feeling that he could not convert the idol worshipping symbol-seeking stubborn stiff-necked people without introducing some symbols, he invented some and named some places as holy, which is against the very grain of his own religious thinking. he ridiculed people who wrongly believed that christ was the son of god. in india, there were no serious philosophers or thinkers before goutama. The elite among the people worshipped elements like air, water etc as gods and propitiated them by burning ghee in fire while chanting some songs in adulation of those gods, in a sophisticated form while common people sacrificed animals and sometimes even human beings, in the crudest form. Goutama opposed all these sacrifices as they were meaningless and inhuman. he was the first great philosopher to deny the existence of any super human being. what he said was that we should live in harmony with laws, physical or biological 'tharmam saranam gachchami, 'we have to live peacefully in a casteless and classless society, sangham saranam gachchaami, and we should adopt a rational and intellectual life. ahimsa is the highest law for the human beings. he was the first environmentalist. we should eschew all acts of violence not because we should love all life like ourselves but because we recognize the right of each and every living thing for a full and fruitful life. buddham saranam gacchami. the supreme law is ahimsa, says yudhistir in answer to yaksha's question. you may think it is like devil quoting scriptures, as your smile indicates. In my opinion ramayan and mahabharat are two of the greatest books in all literature but we do great harm to ourselves and great disrespect to those epics, if we take those stories literally. do you take the imaginative writings of rowling literally? do you believe that some human beings are vampires, as portrayed in stephenie meyer's twilight series? Kalidasa, bhavabhuti and so many other writers after them knew that the characters and events portrayed or narrated in the two great epics were not based on real persons or events. So they altered somewhat or totally changed those characters and incidents to suit the exigencies of their artistic compositions or to reflect the changes in the society after the composition of ramayan or mahabharat. According to mahabharat version, the king coulld not marry except with the approval of his subjects, the people. by kalidasa's time, the king became an autocrat. According to ramayan, sambuka was killed by ram not only in order to bring back a brahmin child to life but also to prevent a sudra from enetring heaven and tainting it with his presence as a result of his illegitimate penances, for which true and valourous deed gods were pleased to shower flowers on ram.

according to bhavabhuti, ram was much pained to kill sambuka as he was obliged to do so by his advisers and sambuka got a place booked for himself in heaven for his true and just penances.

Those who produced films based on the ramayan version of the story, cleverly ignored this episode even though they believed in the infallibility of its author because they feared the indignation of the people if they portrayed this episode, which is one of the dirtiest of its kind in all myths. Goutama was the greatest thinker and philosopher, who has been the main source of inspiration to distinguished Indians like baba saheb ambedkar and his followers and a number of present day existentialist philosophers of the west. this was the country of buddha and the indians were buddhists first and foremost. but idol-loving and symbol-crazy people subverted his philosophy, made him the tenth avatar of their god. goutama never believed in rebirth, let alone avataras. "Einsten the greatest scientist and thinker of the twentieth century said, 'god is, for me, nothing more than the expression and product of human weaknesses, the bible, a collection of honorable yet primitive legends which are nevertheless pretty childish. No interpretation no matter how subtle (for me) changes this. For me the jewish religion like all other religions is an incarnation of the most childish superstitions.'" he explained. Then the man asked the buddha whether or not we should believe in god and worship him and earn merit, if we had to lead a meaningful, rational and intellectual life. the Buddha said to him, 'our search engines, like our rational thinking and the most powerful telescopes we have so far invented have not succeeded in locating god in the known universe and if he exists in the unknown part of the universe, he can in no way decide our fate or affect our fortunes, in which case it is fruitless to worship him. if god is everywhere and in everything, there is no need to look for him or worship him. there is absolutely no need to worship a *sarvavyapi*, or a *sarvantaryami*. god is the greatest invention and the most wonderful invention of the primitive man, who earnestly searched for the first cause. the same invention is proving to be a dead weight, besides inducing the credulous masses to adopt disgraceful attitudes and to indulge in undignified patterns of behavior. Some people walk long distances bare footed, undertake expensive pilgrimages, move around temples on their knees, subject their bodies to extreme physical suffering, fast for days on end or pierce their cheeks, tongues and stomachs and all other parts of their bodies with steel wires, kneel at the feet of the so called holy men or god men and adopt other obnoxious and repulsive modes and attitudes. we are yet to find the first cause, of course, and we may never be able to find the first cause. it has always eluded our efforts. it will always do so in future. i don't think big bang is the first cause. something must have caused the big bang. there is going to be no end to our search. The much touted and the most expensive scientific project to identify the so called god particle may create more questions than answers. our overreaching urge to know all and possess the earth and the universe drives us to open one pandora's box after another. It is useless to wait for godot. we should realize that mankind is helpless before the powerful elements which will one day or other annihilate man, his fantasies and his home, the earth. this is the human condition. We had better face the reality. but people want short-cuts. there is a man in the next street, claiming to be an avatar of god. there is a temple in a far off city.

why should we not earn merit by becoming his devotees or by visiting that temple? these are the meaningless efforts of little minds. they have made gods in their own image, dishonest, ungentlemanly, gloating in self adulation, deriving pleasure in flattery (mukhastuti) from his insincere devotees, purporting to give wealth, health or long life or eternal life after death in the company of ever young and ever beautiful celestial sex workers as quid pro quo. if the telecom ministers do the same thing, you put them in tihar jail. on the other hand you offer praises to your god for doing the same thing. People give names to something which does not exist and then quarrel, fight, shed their blood and that of others over those mere names. you have created gods who demand from you, besides your total devotion, your wealth, your health [you have to stand in a long line in insanitary and unhygienic conditions for hours on end to seek his grace], every part of your body, from your toe nails to your beautiful locks of hair.your god demands donations from you to clear the debts he incurred for several of his marriages. od is a flourishing industry and a roaring business in india. Poor people spend their entire savings to visit his temples and wait hours to have his darshan. Billions of man-hours are wasted in pigrimage, worship and service. rich people elaborately conduct, amidst the chant of vedic mantras, annual nuptials of god, his sons, his grandsons, the products of his normal or gay marriages. they don't leave him alone enjoying even his first night with his one or a bevy of concerts. Your devotional songs are nothing short of pornography, unutterable for a woman, who respects her private parts, to sing. To mention only two so called devotional verses:

[1] *Sreeramanikucha durga vihare,*
[2] *maaraanke ratikelisankularanaarambhe—*
    paurusharasah sthrinam kutah siddhyati.

if we had not been impoverished by these gods, there would have been no poverty in this country. if these god men and these temple trustees sponsor or establish educational and other charitable institutions with a part of their booty, they only do it only to evade taxes or to promote their nefarious businesses. 'how wonderful it would be if there were to be god,' says the principal character in a film.

Christ says, 'consider the lilies of the field. they toil not, neither do they spin but Solomon in all his glory was not arrayed like one of these. Likewise God will feed and clothe the people.' Christ was the first communist who dreamed of a happy world here on the earth without poverty and disease in the kingdom of god. Marx, a non-believer, also like Christ, substituting state in the place of the kingdom of god, dreamed of a happy world sans poverty and sans disease, ignoring the intrinsic corrupt nature of man. his dream was for the establishment of a state which would bring about equality of all but he did not foresee that some men would eventually become more equal than all of the others and that the state also consisted of men who would look after themselves, leaving the poor masses to fend for themselves. God is a myth, a beautiful myth, indeed. One of the characters, in the short story 'putois' written by the great French writer, anatole france, invents, to avoid a persistent unpleasant invitation, an excuse and tells her neighbor that putois, a fictitious person, is expected to work in the garden that day and that is why she cannot attend the party. From that time onwards putois gradually acquires a shape, a character, a profession and a personality in the minds of the villagers as the tale is circulated by word of mouth. the story takes such a firm root in the imagination of the people that finally nobody doubts the existence of putois. The short story illustrates how myths and legends originate, catch the imagination of successive generations of people and influence their minds. myths were intended to satisfy the curiosity of the primitive people concerning why things were what, how and why they were as they were. In the bible there is a beautiful story which explains why there is a running feud between the human beings and the serpents. Myths are mere myths and that is all about them. we have to turn to reality and face the hard facts of our life and our existence on this planet instead of escaping into worlds of myths and fantasies. life is 'a tale told by an idiot, full of sound and fury signifying nothing,' says a character in a famous play.' I came to the earth as a flute only to disappear as thin air into the sky,' says another character in a film,. There are no readymade solutions. Bhagavad gita, hyped to offer solutions to save mankind from the brink of disillusionment, [for man is clinging to a slender rope, seeking footholds on ledges and crevices along a precipice which will ultimately land him on the dead heap of dysfunctional cosmic hardware debris,] is a bundle of contradictions, confounding the confusion in the minds of its readers. In fact, it addresses a small section of warrior class people, now extinct, asking them, to destroy, as a duty, without a thought of the consequences, the enemy, for the victor as well as the vanquished ultimately awaits the same end sooner or later. But the gita does not offer any solution for the masses, who cannot be expected to toil without a thought of the result. It is full of ifs and buts. It says 'you should fight and kill your enemies even whether the soul is to be considered mortal or immortal.' There are many passages in the gita which serve as window-dressing devices to an essentially sectarian and divisive social outlook. It says, 'I am above love and hatred' in one place. At another place it says, 'I am revealing the utmost secret philosophy to you because you are dear to me and as you are a chosen disciple and a cousin of mine.'

At one place it says, 'the well-read brahmin, the cow, the elephant, the dog and low caste person who eats the flesh of a dog should be looked upon and treated equally without discrimination.' At another place, 'it declares, 'I created the fourfold hierarchical caste based social structure,' without even making a mention of those who do not belong to the four castes. Aside from all this, gita is highly ambiguous, each reader, finding their own own explanation, especially, for the core point, namely, the relationship between the hardware, the body and the software, the soul, on the one hand, and the relationship between each local software, the particular soul and the super software, god. the kerala scholar, interpreting the core point, held that the soul is equal to the super soul, the super soul ultimately merging with the soul as they are not different from each other except in intensity. This is like saying 'one is equal to infinity'. the tamil scholar, interpreting the the

same text, held that the soul is quantitatively different from the super soul, ultimately the soul merging with the super soul. Where has it come from in the first place? Why is this

futile journey to and fro? the karnataka scholar, interpreting the same text, held that the soul is different from the super soul and it co-exists with the super soul, depending on the super soul though for its refinement and well-being. The best explanation for the core issue regarding human existence is the most simple, plain, rational and transparent explanation offered by the charvakas. Modifying it in the light of the present scientific knowledge, we can formulate that some fortuitous combination of elements, events and circumstances led to the formation of life on the earth, which entails struggle for survival, for which awareness of the surroundings emerges and from that awareness of itself and its surroundings comes consciousness. From that conscious develops ego which starts alienating itself from its immediate environment. as the life decays and dies owing to accidents beyond its control oron account of its own volition to annihilate itself, or as a result of dysfunctioning of the vital organs due to ware and tare or due to the limitations of the program in its hardware component. with the death o f life, consciousness also dies. This is the hard truth which, though real, is not comforting to the highly evolved and inflated human ego which, as a result, weaves webs of fantasies about soul, god, heaven and eternity. Besides, gita contains patent untruths, the falsity of which was known at the time of propounding the gita itself, like:. rains are the result of the propitiation of the rain god, parjanya, through burning of ghee in the sacrificial fire. as the priests were burning the fat here, American continent was being flooded with continuous rains and tsunamis while people in india suffered from a series of severe droughts, perhaps. For clarity on all of the core questions, again, we have to turn to goutama's philosophy, which advocates a practicable mean, between desire and greed, between self-interest and common good, the common good not only of the humankind but life in general, between a healthy curiosity and an overreaching ambition.' 'Man loves to stride the earth as its possessor and the earth loves to suck him into her gorges', as a poet says in one of his finest songs. 'the earth tells the potter, "how dare you crush me under your feet, the day is sure to come when I shall crush thee under," said kabir, a mystic.

the human condition is portrayed in ramayan thus:

- *niyatihi kaaranam loke niyatihi karma saadhanam*
- *niyatihi sarvabhootaanaam niyogeshviha kaaranam.*
- *Na karta kasyachitkaschinniyogenaapi cheswarah*
- *Swabhave vartate lokastasya kaalah parayanam.*
- *Na kaalah kaalamatyeti na kaalah pariheeyate*
- *Svabhavam cha samasaadya na kinchidativartate.*

This is the quintessence of Buddhism. Human longing for an engagement with eternity is a fond hope for there is no eternity and everything that happens to come into being is subject to change and ultimate death and destruction.therefore each person has to create his own values, acquire new insights, live as far as possible upholding those values and be resilient enough to shed those values as the conditions and circumstances change in the course of time, stop populating the earth at the cost and expense of all other species, recognize and respect the life and well-being of our fellowmen and all other living things around us. We are luckily living in a democratic dispensation, with checks and balances, thanks to ambedkar and others, who drafted our constitution. aside from the general human condition, Indian women and the arab women, notwithstanding the best efforts of raja ramamohamohan ray and periyaar in india and mohammed in arabia, are the victims of the worst exploitation by man. You are the victim of all kinds of illusions, delusions, deceptions and bogeys, my dear young man. But remember your burdens are illusory. once you start thinking and leading a full and meaningful life, guided by reason and science, your liberation and liberty are attainable here on this planet and only on this planet. Scientific ideas unlike religious and philosophical notions are progressive. "what is a progressive idea and what is a retrogressive notion?' asked the man, with a burden on his back. 'progressive ideas are the scientific ideas which put the past behind and look beyond the present. Religious and philosophical notions speculate and put the present and the future behind the past. The religious theories are those which have reached the dead end or which will soon possibly reach the dead end. The progressive ideas are those which work now and work in the conceivable future. The religious notions and scientific ideas may look alike but the basis on which they have been arrived at is what matters. 'the world is one family' or 'we are all children of god' or 'we are all servants of god' are religious notions. 'All life is one' or 'the ecosystem must be protected for the existence and survival of all life' are scientific and progressive ideas which are already proved or are demonstrable now or in the conceivable future. 'we should love all others like ourselves' is a universally proclaimed religious doctrine. 'all others have as much right as we have to have a healthy, peaceful and meaningful life 'is a progressive idea.'

after hearing the buddha's elucidation of life's meaning and purpose e, the man shook off all of his illusions and stood upright and thanked the buddha.

CHAPTER 18

dynamics of communication

english has structures to communicate what the speaker intends to communicate and shade the information that the speaker does not intend to communicate. it has devices to matter-of-factly state, understate as well as overstate thoughts and feelings. though it has a somewhat rigorous word order, it has enough flexibility to permit movement of structures within it for shading, coloring, or highlighting, setting the theme, placing emphasis or focus on a word, phrase or clause. "Studying these aspects of linguistic structures makes one aware of language as a sequentially organized communication in which judicious ordering and placing of emphasis may be important for the proper understanding of the message and its implications" (*The University Grammar of English* by Randolph Quirk et al)

i **ran into John last week at a trade fair in chennai**.(the speaker intends to communicate an event with all the circumstances associated with it. hence simple past tense is used.)

I have run into John recently. (The speaker does not intend to communicate, for whatever reason, the circumstances like the place and time of the event. hence present perfect tense is used.)

he got killed in a street brawl. (semi-passive. slightly colored. he was also responsible for his death.)

he was killed in a train accident. (construction is passive. no color.)

the notorious smuggler was arrested.(passive voice as the focus is on the event and not on the performer.)

119

he was blackmailed by none other than his own brother. (through passive construction, the focus is shifted from the event to the agent of the action.)

john i ran into last week at a trade fair in chennai. (object is moved to the first position for highlighting the theme)**it was John and not kamal that i ran into at a trade fair in chennai.**(a cleft clause is used for focus.).

it was at a trade fair in Chennai that I ran into John. (the focus is on the place of action/event.)

when I last met John, he was working in a private concern in mumbai. (focus is on the independent clause.)

john was working in a private concern in mumbai, when i met him last. (the focus is shifted to the dependent clause.)

Cleft clauses or cloned clauses

we can clone clauses by taking an element of the sentence, we wish to highlight. they are called cleft clauses and are used to lay focus on an element of our choice.

ex. 1.   <u>Ramesh</u> worked <u>in a software company in mumbai</u> before he moved to <u>Chennai</u> <u>to set up his own business.</u>(matrix)

- it was Ramesh, who worked in a software company in Mumbai before he moved to Chennai to set up his own business. • it was in a software company in mumbai that ramesh worked before he moved to chennai to set up his own company.
- it was to chennai that ramesh moved to set up his own factory, after he had worked in a software company in mumbai.
- It was to set up his own business that ramesh moved to chennai, after he had worked in a software company in mumbai.

comment clauses

the speaker or reporter can comment on the message contained in the sentence. they are no w called comment clauses but they are, in actual fact, adverbial clauses. ex. **it was churchill, <u>if i am not wrong</u>, who said that the english sentence is the noblest thing.**

it is the position that determines the function and meaning of not only words and phrases but also clauses in english. ex. **he was a genius, <u>I think</u>**. (comment clause, added as an

afterthought and therefore the speaker is a little bit hesitant and a shade less positive than when he says **i think he was a genius.**(noun clause. its position is fixed) **I think, he was a genius.**(comment clause. its position in the sentence is not fixed.)

this, that, here, there and **it** used as nominal subjects

another important feature of english is the use of **her**e, **there**, **this, that** and **it** as introductory words to prepare the hearer when introducing a new theme or avoiding a clumsy longish subjects. this device is used to help the hearers process the meaning of the communication without much strain on their working memory. examples:-

- **here comes our bus. here is the book you wished to purchase**.
- **there are a number of books in the public library on this subject.**
- **this is my colleague, Rajesh.**
- **that is the reason why I came here.**
- **it is nice to have met you.**
- **it is not as easy to understand poem as to understand a piece of prose passage.**
- **to speak without experiencing a sense of nervousness when preparing to address a huge gathering of a totally unfamiliar audience is well nigh impossible for a debutante orator.**

(It is well nigh impossible—is better.)

- **a very informativebook on socio-linguistics is now available in our college library**. (processing the above construction makes more demand on the working memory than the one that follows. hence the sentence that follows is preferred.)
- **here is now available a very informative book on socio-linguistics in our college library.**
- **"it is hazardous to go on a long trek in this kind of weather."** is better than **"to go on a long trek in this kind of weather is hazardous.)**

it is used as a functional subject when the subject is unclear and when the stem of the verb and the subject is the same. this device, a very productive one, is also a compensatory mechanism in a syntactic situation where any subject, even a nominal subject is necessary to head a well-formed sentence. ex. **it feels good. it is a foul practice. it looks good. itsometimes rains in winter. it snows on the high mountain peaks even in summer months**. if one wants to be cautious and non-committal, one can choose expressions with **it** as a nominal subject, besides the expression **he seems to be guilty** thus: **it seems he is guilty**.

(introductory it) or **he is guilty, it seems**. (a comment clause with **it** as nominal subject.

simple, complex and compound sentences

the messages can be briefly packed into what are called simple sentences, using an **infinitive, participle, a noun phrase** etc. the same messages can be expressed more cogently and clearly in what are called complex sentences with the clause markers such as **because, although, unless** etc. further, the same messages can be conveyed in two or more simple sentences or combined into what are called compound sentences, using the co—coordinating conjunctions such as **and, so, but, or** etc.

he is too erratic in his work to take up a program like this. (simple). **he is so erratic in his work that he cannot take up a program like this**. (complex) **he is very erratic in his work. He cannot take up a program like this**. (two sentences) **he is erratic so he cannot take up a program like this.**(Compound) **please be kind enough to attend my sister's wedding.**(simple) **will you be so kind as to attend my sister's**

wedding. (complex) **please be kind. please attend my sister's wedding. (two sentences) Please be kind and attend my sister's wedding.** (compound sentence) the best way to convey this message is through a simple sentence.

standing at the main entrance, the bride and bridegroom received the guests. (simple)

two successive actions casually related but not specifically connected by reason, or cause and consequence are not expressed in a complex sentence without suggesting some meaning extraneous to the text. ex. **going to the window, he looked at the traffic on the road.** the best way to convey this information is through a compound sentence. **The bride and bridegroom stood at the main entrance and received the guests. He went to the window and looked at the traffic on the road.**

having been rescued by the coast guard in time, he luckily escaped a certain death.

(simple) **he escaped a certain death because he had been rescued in time by the coast guard.** (Complex) **The coast guard rescued him in time so he escaped a certain death.**

(Compound) **the coast guard rescued him in time. So he escaped a certain death.** (two sentences)

because of his hard work and efficiency he was promoted as the general manager. For want of quorum, the meeting was adjourned to the next working day. (simple sentences) **because he was efficient and hard—working he was promoted as the general manager.** (Complex) **he was efficient and hard-workingand therefore he was romoted as the general manager.** (Compound) **He was efficient and hard-working. and so he was promoted as general manager. as there was no quorum, the meeting was adjourned to the next working day.** (complex) **there was no quorum and so the meeting was adjourned to the next working day.** (Compound) **there was no quorum. the meeting was adjourned to the next working day.**

in spite of his injury, he won the match.(Simple)though he suffered from an injury, he won the match. (Complex) **He suffered from an injury and yet he won the match.**

(Compound) **He suffered from an injury. However, he won the match.**

in the event of your failing to pay the rent before the end of the month, you must vacate the flat. (simple) **if you fail to pay the rent before the end of the month, you must vacate the flat. (Complex) pay the rent before the end of the month or vacate the flat. (compound) pay the rent before the end of the month. if not you have to vacate the flat.**(two sentences)

We can follow any order in simple and complex sentences but we must follow chronological or logical order of cause /reason and effect in a compound sentences. ex. **he waited until the arrival of the train. Until the arrival of the train he waited. He waited until the train arrived. Until the train arrived, he waited. (But) The train arrived and he waiteduntil its arrival.**

in spite of the somewhat rigorous word order imposed by its syntax, the english sentence is flexible enough to permit movement of structures within it for focus and emphasis, which is why english, in the hands of its exponents, is capable of communicating every nuance of tone, feeling or thought.

exercise 25.

Convert the following sentences to simple sentences.

- idon'tknowwhenthetrainarrives.
- this ash, when it is mixed with lime, acquires cement-like properties.
- for those who harbor the rankling fear about the end of the printed word in this electronic age, a visit to the Chennai book fair is a great source of satisfaction.
- rabindranath tagore, w ho won the nobel prize for literature in 1913, was also a painter.
- though he worked hard, he failed to score high grades in the test.

- in case you are innocent, you will be honorably acquitted.
- we will fulfill whatever we promise.
- he didn't score such high grades as he could win a scholarship.
- the defect in the glass was so glaring that anyone could notice it.
- as he was exonerated from all charges of corruption, he is now reinstated in his previous position.
- it was owing to his perseverance that that he succeeded in every enterprise he undertook.
- the moment you reach the place, give me a call.
- first consider the offer carefully and then accept it.
- you may be industrious but you may sometimes fail in your enterprises.
- walk straight, turn left at the fourth cross road, reach the end of the street, turn left. there, you will find a red building to your left.

exercise.26.

rewrite the following as complex sentences.

- there was no evidence to convict him and so he was discharged.
- she was not only an efficient engineer but was also an able administrator.
- either clear your debts within a month or face prosecution.
- he was eligible but he was not selected.
- he had enough money and he could pay the bill.
- he went to the station and by that time the train had departed.
- the matter was being discussed in the council meeting and at that time he was visiting his brother in the u. s. a.
- leave me alone and if you do so I promise to help you.
- he was very inefficient and so he could not be promoted.
- iwillcomebackhereand pleasewaithereuntilthen.
- come here immediately after finishing your work.
- idon'tknowhiswhereabouts.
- do you know the reason for his absence?
- don't wait here for me if I fail to come before noon.
- Thanks are due to all of you for your assistance for making this function a grand success.

exercise 27.

rewrite the following as compound sentences.

- if you do not cooperate with me, you have to resign from the committee.
- as there is not enough evidence to convict him, he is set free.
- isawhimfleeingfromtheplaceofcrime.
- searching his residence, we did not find any material evidence connecting him to the crime.
- we will compensate you the loss you have suffered during this risky operation.
- when he opened the steel bureau, he found it empty.
- the kidnappers demanded rs. one million as ransom for the safe release of their son.
- the day, being rainy with squally winds, the children were not allowed to go out to play.
- since tomorrow is a public holiday, no shop will be open.
- although she was irregular in her work, she was not taken to task.

exercise 28.

use introductory **there** or **it** as the nominal subject and rewrite the following sentences.

- an envelope is on the table.
- to keep a house spick and span is the duty of the housekeeper.
- that he embezzled the money has been proved beyond a reasonable doubt.
- it appears there is no doubt about his involvement.
- where you are going and what you are doing is not my concern.
- a motive has tobethereforeverycrime.

A beautifulcarpet iso nthefloor.

- speaking impolitely is not good manners.
- remembering the name of customer who occasionally visits the shop is not possible.
- there appears to be a number of solutions to the problem.

- what you do with the money is not my concern.
- they believed that the judge, who was caught accepting a bribe in a sting operation, committed suicide.

exercise. 29.

clone cleft clauses from the matrix sentences given below.

- rakesh sharma was the Indian astronaut who travelled around the earth in a russian spacecraft.
- i purchased this book yesterday in a used book shop on the mount road.
- our friend narrated this story to us when we were travelling in a train to madurai.
- the material evidence alone is sufficient to prove him guilty.
- an ordinary police officer successfully investigated this case which the cbi could not solve for years.

CHAPTER 19

language and culture

language reflects the culture and the living conditions of its native speakers. england is a cold country for the best or the worst part of the year and so the people love and celebrate summer and the warmth it brings into their lives. summer days are long and **warm. warm greetings, warm welcome, warm reception and warm hospitality** sound quite agreeableand pleasant to british ears whereas**cold and cool** indicate cruelty, frigidity or at least lack of friendliness. of course, we all welcome a cool breeze on a warm day in India as well as in britain. **cold comfort, cool and calculating, keeping one's cool, cool customer** are expressions used to show discomfort or lack of friendliness or emotion. quite contrarily, expressions with the words **cool** or **cold** in Indian languages evoke feelings of affection and friendliness. **hot** is used to refer to items of food and strong feelings and not normally to temperature in English. a bright and sunny day in england is a hot and scorchingday in india. it is ridiculousto say "**it is very warm today,**" when the mercury is hoveringbetween 43 and 44 degrees celsius in india.

language reflects the way of life, the insights and the broad contours of the culture of its native speakers, which is why we should not let any living language die, even if it is spoken by a small community. oral communication systems have taken different roads in their development and we would be losers if we could not, at least in our imagination, travel back the roads they had once taken to reach the present stage.

culture in its crudest and lowest manifestations, pandering to the basic human instincts and sentiments like regional or linguistic chauvinism, is known to divide people but in its noblest and highest manifestations attains universality, creating an inclusive human culture to unite and respect all life. culture and myths shape the human perceptions regarding natural phenomena and these perceptions are reflected in speech. every day **the sun appears or is reborn** in India and he **disappears or dies** every day after scorching the earth, which is consistent with the popular Indian myths. It is **sunrise** and **sunset** in the little islands of great britain. fire had to be stolen from heaven, according to a popular greek myth whereas earth and fire are inalienable elements along with water, air and sky in India.

the english language shows that the natives of Great Britain have had no great experience of a joint family, for their familial relationships are, for all practical purposes, limited to father, mother, brother, sister, and probably grandparents. all others are uncles, aunts and the gender insensitive, convenient hold-all word **cousins.** of course; they have step-brothers and half sisters aplenty. Nevertheless, they have words to connect themselves, though matter—of—factly, to the remotest relatives. they have first, second, third etc. up to billionth cousin in the wilds of africa, chimpanzee. besides, they have cousins, not once or twice but dozens of times removed. they have brotherhood and sisterhoodto forge fellowship or professional relationship with people living in the remotest places on the planet. we have only brothers and sisters in india. when we refer to our cousins in India, we are inclined to say cousin brother or cousin sister, which for purists is a contradiction in terms. a cousin is a cousin when he/she is not one's brother or sister. brother and sister as well as sibling may pass into oblivion if one one child for one couple norm is adopted throughout the world. but cousin will be good currency as long as family system lasts. oald classifies **cousin brother** as indian english instead of acknowledging it as a useful contributionto the english language.if we come across a statement such as, "**he got married to his own cousin,**" how do we know whether it is a gay marriageor a normal one?

In english it is **uncle** whether he is father or mother's brother, **aunt** whether she is father or mother'ssister. we have, in south Indian languages, different words for father's elder brother and younger brother, for mother's elder sister and younger sister. a lecturer in one of the indian languages once caused the audience to burst into an uncontrollable fit of laughter when he, speakingin english, perhaps for the first time, referred to his father's younger brother as "my younger father." of course, he merely translated the phrase from his native language.

he could not hide his blushes when his friends pointed out to him why the audience laughed.

there are single words in south Indian languages for **elder brother** and **elder sister**, showing how the native speakers of these languages hold their elders in high regard. they have also words for each elder brother and elder sister, if there are more than one and even if they have more than a dozen. there are also single words for younger brother and younger sister who are affectionately addressed likewise. there are different words in these languages for **ripe fruit** and **raw fruit**. by the by, do you know what the English call the fruit after the skin, pips, seeds or stones are removed? **flesh,** which in indian languages is only what remains after the skin and bones are removed from an animal.

Theoretically english people have very ideal marital relationships, though the marriage system as a whole is crumbling everywhere in the world, more so in england. your wife or husband's brother, sister, mother, father are your brother, sister etc. husband and wife are one and inseparable, in theory though.In Tamil also, daughter-in—law is rightly called another daughterand the son-in—law, another son or highly respected son.

Idiom, a product of cultural, climatic and socio-economic conditions in which the native speakers live, presents some problems to the Indian students of English. 'an idiom can be defined as a number of words, which when taken together, have a different meaning from the individual meaningof each word.' ("English idioms" by Jennifer Seidl) an idiom is an expression peculiar to a particular language and we cannot literally translate it into other languages. for example, 'our magazine is available in all four shops' means in any other language it is available only in four shops but in tamil it means it is available in all shops. To give another example, the telugu idiomatic expression,' I don't know whether you will drown me in milk or water but you are my refuge' means in telugu, 'I am in dire straits. I don't know whether you will render me help or leave me in the lurch. however you are my sole refuge.' translated into any other language literally, it means, 'i am unconcerned whether you will kill me by drowning me in milk or in water. I am solely at your mercy.'

some idioms in english are easy to understand, particularly those with comparisons like **as busy as a bee**, **as clear as crystal** etc. however some idioms like, **run the gauntlet, flog a dead horse, hold your horses** are not only difficult to understandbut stale and worn—out. every languagehas its own idiom. as interpolatingthe idiom of one languageinto another makes a discourse not only bizarre but also totally incomprehensible, the Indian speakers of english should desist from the temptationof translatingthe idiom of their native languageinto english. now that English has attained a preeminentposition, with a truly global reach, the users of the languageshould prefer to use plain english instead of the garbled expressionsof a bygone age. it is better to use **a trial run** instead of **a dry run, honest** instead of **above board, in a state of anxiety and suspense** instead of **on the tenterhooks, get down to practicable aspects** instead of **get down to brass tacks**. my readers, if there are any, will, i suspect, take my advice with a pinch of salt.

High—brow idiom has a low-brow cousin, slang, into whose company one should not fall, if one wants to be respectable in one's speech. but many of the idioms have their origin in slang. '**gas**, the american slang, meaning "idle useless voluble talk," has travelled a long distance to reach the Indian shores to become a part of the common parlance among our youth. '**bullshit,**' or its shortenedform, '**shit,**' an american slang, is now universally heard in respectablecircles. '**bullshit**'stands for 'something useless' even in india but 'cow dung' is considerd precious by some members of a communityof people. In fact, slang gives a touch of peculiar slangy flavor to any discourse and it often finds a respectable place in the writingsof even well-known authors.

today's slang or jargon will be tomorrow's idiom. the computer jargon like **netizen, hack, ram, home site** have already become commonexpressions.'**a bird in hand, a stitch in time, house-hunting, brokering peace, a square peg in a round hole** have an unenviable descent. some idioms have come from ancient epics or works of famous writers or from observationof natural phenomena.Examples:—**midas touch, pandora'sbox, the salt of the earth, sour grapes, caviar to the general, Jekyll and hyde, crocodile tears, have ants in your pants, litmus test** etc. **Indian English is** replete with expressionslike **brahmin, housewife, house warming[house wife is** now being replaced by **homemaker,**(north american origin)], **four twenty, god man, god promise, marriage broker, masaala cinema, build-up, for long no see, cat on the wall policy, living like a frog in a well** etc.

english has such innumerable phatic expressionslike **hello, hi, excuse me, beg pardon, bye, nice day, nice meeting, how do you do, you see, i see, see you, damn it** and greetings for every time of the day and the night and for every important occasion in life, as to make social life run smoothly like a well-oiled machine. Now all these expressions have become common currency, inexpensive yet cheeringexpressionsuttered to lift one another'sspirits in the otherwise drab mechanical every day social existence of people throughout the world.

Exercise27

. rewrite the following sentences in simple and plain

English.

1. fielding is the achilles' heel of the Indian cricket team.
2. the investment that he received from a private company when his father was the chief minister, is now the albatross round his neck.
3. you can' t live with a spouse who blows hot and cold over everything all the time of the day.
4. the former telecom minister has many a skeleton in his cupboard/ closet.
5. she always keeps a stiff upper lip as she was brought up by highly snobbish parents.,
6. he was given the sack as he mocked at his boss's stammering speech
7. this boy is the chip off the old block. look at his snub nose.
8. your girl friend is a real looker, though not a beauty.
9. the super star has been my buddy from school days.
10. he started singing as the cops subjected him to the third degree.

krishna

The following episode illustrates how economics and politics determine social traditions, mores and customs.

(the events of the following play will take place in the 25th century when there will be a mere five hundred females for every thousand males, what with the killing of female fetuses, dowry deaths, female suicides and murders related to dowry and gang rapes in the centuries that precede.

[Enter preetha and nakul]

Preetha: what happened to sahadev today? He used to come home before five every day. Is he still in the playing field? He has left his cell phone on the dining table. Why don't you, nakul, ring up one of his friends and find out the whereabouts of your brother?

Nakul: don't worry, mum. Nothing will have happened to your beloved son. May be he is still playing tennis. Here he is, mom.

Preethi: why are you so late, my dearest boy? I was so worried.

Saha: there is good news for you, mom. I played the best match of my life. How wonderful! I have brought a beautiful gift home.

Preethi: excellent. I know you are a lucky boy. I heartily congratulate you. Whatever is the gift you brought home today like ever before, you have got to share it with your elder brother, in accordance with our family convention.

Saha: you are mistaken, mom. This is not a gift to be shared. Come in, Krishna [he shouts]

[Krishna enters]

This lovely girl is the gift I am talking about. She will be a member of our family from today. Her father is a big shot, an industrialist. She is also an entrepreneur by her own right. She is a genius. She is her dad's only daughter.

Preethi: did her father agree to this marriage proposal, rich as he is supposed to be?

Saha: her father himself arranged the tennis match to decide a life partner for his daughter. Our cousin, dhrit and me courted her for the last one year. Her father arranged a match between me and dhrit. The winner was to take her hand. I won the match handsomely, 4sets to 1.

Preethi: this sounds like an episode in mythology. I cannot believe it. anyhow your talent has won for you a marvelous gift. I have already said that you should share with nakul whatever gift you have brought home. That is my word.

Saha: this is something from a myth. That is fiction, mom, and this is real life. It is impossible.

Nakul: what sahadev says is right, mom. What you suggest is preposterous. I cannot agree to this.

Preethi: nothing doing. I stick to my word. She is a bride for you both. You know what the sex ratio in our country is at present? There are a mere 500 females for every 1000 males. You love each other, don't you? You are twins. You should remain together all your life in a joint family. Unity is strength, you know. That was precisely why kunthi got all her five sons married to the same girl. If each of her sons had decided to marry separately and set up families of their own, they could never have regained their father's right to rule the country. It was her strategy more than expediency. Of course, at that time as it is now men outnumber women by two to one. We have to change according to the conditions of our times. For instance we are minimalists in all respects. Do you know who the prime minister of our country is, nakul?

Nakul: no, I have no idea, mom.

Preethi: you are right. In fact, it is not necessary to know. People used to depend on the governments even for food in those days whereas our governments if there are any at present depend on us. We produce our power ourselves. every homestead has a water recycling plant. People used to be slaves of not only of their traditions but also of their politicians. We eat without becoming slaves of food. We speak without becoming slaves of our language.

Sahadev. I read somewhere, mom, they didn't use to play games at all. They used to watch others play games. They used to bet on the matches played by some professionals and the results of the matches were fixed by book makers before they were actually played. How idiotic those people were!

Nakul: they used to have film stars and those film stars used to have fans and fan clubs. Voyeurism was a cult with them in every sphere of their life. They lived in slums but they lavishly celebrated the successes of their heroes in politics or films.

preethi: they used to worship gods and goddesses. They used to celebrate the nuptials of their deities with pomp and exuberance. We have changed. We are very much different than them. They indulged in self adulation. They used to sing songs like 'our country is better than the entire world. Our language is greater than all other languages. We have high mountains and long rivers which reverberate with the praises of our deity.' They fetishized names, places, animate and inanimate objects and quarreled over those petty things. They built excellent structures to house their gods while their poor lived in uninhabitable and unhygienic holes. they were vainglorious and stupid and to top it all they were proud of their stupidity. Poor people used to end their lives unable to clear their debts while their rich amassed wealth brazenly through corrupt and dishonest methods. They replaced monarchy by family rule. They replaced the rule of law by the rule of the muscle and the money. We have saved the institution of marriage which was vitiated by murky financial dealings. My dear boys, you must promise to me that you both accept my advice and share this girl as your wife.

Nakul: mother wants to spare the trouble of searching a bride for me. she thinks, tardy as I am, I can never win the hand of a girl in the present intensely competitive marriage market.

Preethi: that is one of the reasons, of course. Nakul is an introvert. He is so self-conscious. Our family finances are in a pretty bad shape at the moment. I know this pretty child won't inherit anything as her father's property goes to the state when he passes away, in accordance with our law. Both of you have to join a university for higher studies this year. Of course, only if this gorgeous beauty endorses my proposal. What, my child, will you have nakul also as your husband? In actual fact, nakul is more handsome than sahadev, though not as talented. I assure you he will be a nice husband for you.

Krishna: I have no objection, ma'm, I mean mom, I mean my sweet mother-in—law. I am delighted. It is like two birds at one shot as they say. I remember an incident from my childhood days. I was brought up with two of my cousins. Which one of your cousins will you marry? My mother used to ask me. At that time I was only eight. My answer was always the same. I would marry them both, I used to reply innocently.

(Nakul and sahadev embrace krihna as their mother looks on happily.)

CHAPTER 20

spelling and pronunciation

one of the most problematic features of english is its spelling. pronunciation and spelling are such a mismatch as one needs to allocate two separate folders in one's brain to avoid pitfalls in either speaking or writing. it is ironical that, in spite of the intentions and the efforts of the best minds, english spelling remains a nightmare even to the experienced practitioners of the language, though the task of simplifying it is, by no means, daunting.

Simplification of spelling can be accomplished at the blink of a little rodent by using the present day technology. many specious arguments are advanced to retain the conventional spelling, a luxury which bestows no real advantage, while entailing enormous unnecessary altogether avoidable effort on the part of the learner and the expert alike.

pronounce the following words:

charm—chute—charisma, buffet—buffet, idol—idle, gills—ginger, fugitive—frugal
certain—curtain, bright—brittle, metal—mettle, always—almond, cell—sell, take—teak, reign—rain—reins, fined—find, mined—mind, envelope—envoy—entrepreneur, suit—suite—soot, live—live.

reforming the spelling is easy enough and that too without adding a single new letter to the existing alphabet. It is not necessary to adopt international phonetic alphabet for the purpose. we can delete the three letters, c, q and x which represent no particular sounds.

we can also safely delete the punctuation mark, apostrophe. the upper case letters can be dispensed with as well, for they give little advantage while demanding unnecessary extra attention and labor. in fact, there is no corresponding device in speech for the capitalization of proper names or apostrophe mark. most of the languages have none of these conventions. in german, every noun is capitalized for no obvious advantage.

Thefollowing letters and their combinations will suffice to make the spelling quite adequately reflect the speech sounds.

The consonant sounds (24)

ch even now normally represents the sound as in the word chick and it can continue to represent the same sound. **dh, sh, ng, th, zh** can represent the sounds in the words **that, show, thing, think, pleasure** respectively, the rest of the letters, representing the same sounds as they do now. **G, j** and **y** will represent the sounds in the words **go, judge** and **yes** as they do mostly at present.

vowel sounds (17).**a, e i, o, u** can represent the vowel sounds as in the words **but, bed, sit, got** and **put** respectively. **aa, ae, ee, oo** can represent the sounds as in the words **father, bat, teeth**, and **pool** in that order.

ei, ou, ai, oi, au, ia, ea, ua can represent the sounds as in the words **may, go, kite, boy**, **now, here, hair** and **pure** respectively.

Exercise28.

rewrite the following poem, using the method explained above, to reasonably reflect the way we read the same.

of travelling by different roads

On the terrace of my building one winter eve I met a dove,
Who looked pretty cute and i greeted her with a bow.
we both share the same protoplasm from primeval amoeba and we are distant cousins, both hailing from aquaba.

I lost all the old skills i inherited from mother nature,
While she retains them all unlike me, a poor helpless creature.
She never depends on a realtor or a carpenter,
an architect or a plumber to build her a cozy shelter.
needing no beauticians, perfumeries or fashion dressers,
she always, as though coming fresh out of a bandbox, saunters
on the parapet with silky soft grey neck and black wings,
brown feathers for a tail, sporting at her back two black rings.
She strolls elegantly with dainty little feet painted light red
a white beauty spot, to boot, on her beak, sharp and pointed,
Two pinky spots for eyes, stealing glances at me, a subtle predator,
belonging to the race which breeds many a poacher, despoiler and hunter.

She has no nagging fears about the morrow,
no traces of sad memories from the past on her brow,
for she feels the pain or the joy only out of the present moment,
Her curiosity, being confined to her immediate environment.
the seconds before or after the big bang or the little whimpers of god particle
in the tube which swallowed tax payers' billions of pounds, do not in her mind rankle. What if the sun dies, giving up the ghost, reappearing as a red monster, With an over—bloated body, crushing the little earth in his deadly encounter?

What if the sun and his car fitted with a seven—horse—powered engine
with all his entourage is gobbled up by a mysterious black hole?
These and a host of nightmarish thoughts do my sleep and siesta ruin
and put paid to my fond hopes of engagement with eternity withal.

Every wakeful hour I am hampered by traffic snarls, jams and the cop Waiting to rob me at every road corner whenever on the yellow line I stop, whereas she wings her way freely through sheer instinct in the sky's highway, With no compass or google maps to help her on the right course to stay.

She has no god to put up who she needs to erect a huge resplendent building, while her poor homeless human cousins, who put more faith in the hoary fictions

of the past than solid scientific facts or the teachings of goutama or simple reasoning
being slaves of outmoded traditions, obsolete social norms, sops and free rations
provided by crafty politicians, dwell on pavements to populate and defecate
or just keep their bones, flesh and fluid together in unhygienic dirty slums to replicate.
She's a lord of life, a free bird in the true sense of the phrase,
for pelf, name or fame, with no unquenchable craze,
no propensity to garner or hoard grain by foul means or shady tactics
in order to provide for her progeny's progeny's—progeny 's chicks.

CHAPTER 21

varieties of english

(In the doctor's consultation room)

john: may I come in, doctor?

Doctor prasad: ender, please.

john: i came to chennai to die in the morning.

doctor : I am sorry, really sorry. it must be some terminal illness.

john: no, doctor, nothing of that sort. i am a plier.

doctor: what kind of trade do you ply?

john: i am a tennis plier. tennis tournament starts tomorrow in this city, you see.

doctor: ah! i understand. i love tennis. will you be seaded?

john: no, am notseeded, I endered the tournament through a wild card.

Doctor: what I mean is take your sead, please.

john: thank you, doctor. i must be hundred per cent fit to ply tomorrow's match. i feel a bit uneasy here, in my stomach. may be indigestion.

Doctor: wader condamination, no doubt. p.p is all right. give this prescription to the nurse in the dispensary. by tomorrow morning you will be fit as a fiddle.

john: thanks a lot.

at the dispensary

nurse : here is the pill. Pay the pill at the cash counter.

John: have i got to give this pill at the cash counter?

nurse: no, no. You take this pill. pay the doctor's pill, money in the front office.

John: thanks.have a nice die, young woman.

(nurse is speechless.)

there are at least three major varieties of english, aside from the indian variety or varieties, for that matter. they differ from one another in spelling, pronunciation and vocabulary, though there are no big differences in grammar, for no speaker of any one of these varieties follows any grammar whatsoever in their day-to-day business of life.

american English is closer to indian english, particularly in pronunciation. the words **father** and **saw** are pronounced as faather and saa. The medial "r", not followed by vowel sound is pronounced in american variety though not as distinctly as in indian variety. Our "**go, drove, trove**" sound more american than british. sometimes indian speakers of english pronounce, like british, **ask, mask, task** etc. as **aask, maask** taask etc. or like the americans as aesk, maesk, taesk etc. t-tapping or voicing 't' in certain situations occurring in american and australian varieties is virtually absent from spoken english throughout india except in tamilnadu.

australian **ei** in **day, may, play** is pronounced as **ai** as in **die, my** and **ply**. like the british, we say **laugh and, aunt**, but the americans pronounce the words as **laef, aent**.

142

we broadly follow british spelling though american spelling may eventually replace both the indian and the british varieties as microsoft and other office tools we are used to, adopt the easier and simpler american spelling.

however, american english differs from the british variety in respect of some words and their usage. for example, we say dr. manmohan Singh government but americans say obama administration. the american equivalent of the indian and the british word "government" is "administration". we drive cars, the british, motor cars, the americans, automobiles. we, like americans, use the word 'kerosene', which is the british equivalent of paraffin. we say, like the british and the americans 'genuine' but australians and new zealanders say 'dinkum'

a list of words and phrases peculiar to Indian variety of English is given below with their equivalents in british and american varieties.

Indian

aero plane	aero plane	airplane
aluminium	aluminium	aluminum
antenna	aerial	antenna
autumn	autumn	fall
bio-data	curriculum	resume
biscuit	biscuit	cookie
Book shop	Book shop	bookstore
car	motor car	Car, automobile
carriage	carriage	car(train)
chips	chips	french fries
curtains	curtains	drapes
dial tone	dialing tone	dial tone
diversion	diversion	detour
dustbin	dustbin	ashcan
Engine driver	Engine driver	engineer
flat	flat	apartment
Goods train	Goods train	Freight train
government	government	administration
Ground floor	Ground floor	First floor
guard	guard	conductor

hoarding	hoarding	billboard
Hold all	Hold all	carryall
holiday	holiday	vacation
kerosene	paraffin	kerosene
lift	lift	elevator
luggage	luggage	baggage
maize	Maize, sweet corn	corn
maths	maths	math
Medical shop	pharmacist	druggist
Mum, mummy	Mum, mummy	Mom, mommy
nappy	nappy	diaper
note	note	bill
Notice board	Notice board	Bulletin board
petrol	petrol	gasolene
Post code	Post code	Zip code
queue	queue	line
Ring road	Ring road	beltway

CHAPTER 22

Story telling

of gods and god men

Story telling is, perhaps, the oldest art. Every mother tells a story to lull her child to sleep. Grandparents, before watching TV and browsing internet became the hobbies and Preoccupations of the young and the old alike, used to tell stories to their grandchildren, who sat around them in long summer evenings, to educate, entertain and train them to face the world. We are all, to start with, exposed to the reality through the fictional events in the mainstream or folk literature. There are many ways of telling a story. For example, the following story is in a question and answer form.

- Why did the regular patrons of a tea stall, on the highway, go, one day, without their early morning cup that cheered and prepared them for their daily chores?
- because the milkmaid, who used to supply milk to the tea stall, did not do so that morning.
- Why didn't she supply milk to the tea stall?
- because the cow did not give milk. Why didn't the cow give milk?
- because the cowherd did not take it out to the village common for grazing the previous day.
- Why didn't the cowherd take out the cow for grazing?
- because his mother didn't prepare his breakfast. Why didn't his mother prepare his breakfast?
- because his mother had to pamper and pacify his baby sister, who was crying all the morning.
- Why was the baby sister crying?
- because an ant bit her little finger.

- Why did the ant bite the baby?
- when the story teller asked the ant why it had bitten the baby, which was why, eventually, the patrons of the tea stall had to go without their daily morning tea, the ant said, "do you expect me to simply suffer when a brat pokes its silly nose in my affairs and insert its little finger in my hole?"

The same story can be narrated thus:

one morning a little baby inserted its little figure in an ant hole

The storytelling is like constructing an edifice, the auther, building it brick by brick, plastering and painting it, decorating its interiors tastefully, so as to attract and sustain the interest of the listeners. The storyteller may build up suspense till the end or narrate the events in the order of their occurrence. The story, as the bard says, may "hold a mirror up to nature" or take the listeners to a world of fantasy.

But a story, to succeed, should sound authentic. Now read the following story and rewrite it in the reverse order.

The death and life of aanand baba (ardhnaari), the gay god man

The death of ardhnaari, the gay god man, was as phenomenal and mysterious as was his life. The thing, embellished with flowers of every color and fragrance, embalmed with expensive imported scents and native sandal paste, couched in a freezer, kept in the vast prayer hall of the ashram in order to facilitate foreign and indian dignitaries and devotees to pay their last respects, was not the dead body of the self-proclaimed god man at all. In actual fact, it was not the dead body of any man or the carcass of any beast. It was a waxwork figure which was covered with flower wreaths and sandal sticks. Only the visage of the figure, created in the exact image of ardhnaari's face, was made visible. When and of what did the god man die? What happened to his dead body? Was he brutally murdered or did he die of slow poisoning? What did the perpetrators of the heinous crime intend to achieve by putting an untimely end to the baba's life?

Satyam, alias ardhnaari alias aanand baba, the eldest child of goutham and ahalya, was born like any other child. No star appeared to guide his worshippers to the place of his birth and no comet heralded his birth. He was born hardly seven months after the marriage of goutham with ahalya. At first goutham satisfied himself thinking that the child was delivered prematurely. But a suspicion lurked in his mind that the child had been conceived as a result of his wife's fling with her maternal uncle, indra, who the child closely resembled. Satyam was the eldest of five siblings, a brother and twin sisters, kaveri and ganga. his father never treated him with as much love and affection as he did the other children. There was another reason for this. Satyam was often called a dunce and was caned by his teachers for his poor performance in studies. He remained glued to the same bench and the same class while his younger brother overtook him and got promoted to a higher class. He absented himself most of the time from school as he dreaded his class teacher. He often hid his school bag in a dunghill near the school and roamed in the village common during the school hours. dunce though he was in studies, he was given to daydreaming and wild imagination. When he was five years old, he planted a one rupee silver coin, stolen from his father's pocket, in the backyard of the small thatched hut, where his parents, who led a hand to mouth existence with five children, lived. He fancied that the coin would sprout and grow into a tree and yield one rupee coins which would wipe away the poverty of his parents, who mortgaged a couple of acres of dry land, their only ancestral property, to bring up their children. Satyam received severe hiding for this from his father. Satyam's only hobby was attending dramas staged in the street corners, puppet shows and harikathas (god's stories told by a singer) in the nearby town. He imagined that one day he would grow strong like hanuman and toss the school teacher with his cane to a place beyond the seven seas. God took the form of a human being to scourge the evil doers. Perhaps, he was himself an avatar of vishnu or saibaba. Two events supported his conceit that he was born to accomplish a divine purpose. Once he fell nearly twelve feet down a Palmyra tree into a thorny bush. He escaped with only minor bruises. One day when he was returning from the nearby town after attending a harikatha performance of Krishna dancing on the hoods of kaliya, a mythical serpent, he stepped on what he thought a serpent in the dark of the night. The snake turned quickly round and opened its hood, he imagined, but moved away quietly without harming him. Though no love lost between satyam and his father, he loved his brother and sisters. But one incident changed his life and forced him to leave home. One afternoon his father saw his younger brother on top of satyam in a sex act in imitation of their father and mother who performed a similar act every night after their children were supposed to have gone to sleep. His father thrashed satyam and ordered him to leave home for good, in spite of the pleading and begging of his mother to spare the boy, who was just twelve at that time. Ganga followed him for some distance crying bitterly and bade him a tearful farewell.Thus satyam had to leave home and wander from town to town searching for work and some times begging for food. He worked in hotels as a server. He had a stint as a carpenter's apprentice, a barber's help and a compounder's assistant in a clinic. he frequently felt the pangs of hunger. He blamed his fate for not giving him a comfortable home and a steady job. When he was working as a sales boy at a medical shop in madras, one day, he witnessed shokro's magic show. He was so fascinated by the bengali babu's magic performance that he met him after the show and begged him to take him as his apprentice. From then on satyam travelled with the magician from one city to another and learnt hypnotism and many tricks performed with the sleight of hand.During their shows in delhi, satyam was shocked to see carcasses of goats or sheep in display at the entrance of non-vegetarian hotels in the main streets of pahargunj, leading to the new delhi railway station. He loved non-vegetarian food but after seeing such repulsive exhibition of dead bodies, he not only vowed to give up non-vegetarian food but never from that time onwards ate food in what were euphemistically called military hotels.

During his stay in Calcutta, he came under the influence of communism, particularly its rationalist outlook. His guru was also a rationalist and so he also became a rationalist As a boy he fervently believed in the existence of god. His most fancied god was vekateswara, believed to be mahavishnu. As a boy he frequently visited temples. He relished *prasadam*, particularly, *paramaannam*, rice cooked with jiggery, which the temple priest used to distribute grudgingly and stingily to the hungry poor children. The waifs and strays of the village flocked to the temple on Saturday mornings and waited hours for that measly but mouth—watering heavenly *paramannam*.

Satyam learnt bengali and english from his guru, shokro, who had a good collection of books on history, economics, politics, religion, philosophy and science, besides literary works of great english and sankrit authors. He avidly broused those books and he held discussions with shokro on the questions of life and death.

all natural things, satyam now believed, have natural causes. we are not able to find causes for so many things. Perhaps we may or we may not find answers to all the natural phenomena. People believe in god and fate to fall back upon the former in times of dire need or to conveniently blame the latter for their shortcomings and failures. god is many things to many people, a symbol, an enigma, an abbreviation, a colon, a semicolon and a question mark or a last stop. it is not man who was made in the image of god. it was god who was made in the image of man, with all his weaknesses, arrogant in success, egotistical, eager to flatter for receiving favors, being himself susceptible to flattery, capable of corrupting the environment and subverting the purpose of the institutions he has himself made.

When shokro was residing in Calcutta, satyam used to stay in shokro's house in kalighat. Shokro was a widower. his fiteen year old daughter, debyoni, stayed in a boarding school while his son, about the same age as satyam, lived with his father and some times accompanied him during his travels in india and abroad. Satyam used to share bijoy's bed room while he stayed with his guru in Calcutta. On one such occasion, shokro and his son went to their native village near calcutta to attend a relative's marriage. satyam was alone in the house when debyoni dropped in, to spend her weekend. She was pleasantly surprised to see satyam alone in the house. Satyam shared the supper he had prepared for himself with debyoni and retired to his bed for the night. As the rain started buffeting the tiled roof of the old house pitter-patter, the November nippy night became more chilly, bebyoni, entered his bed room and sat on his bed, to satyam's surprise and discomfort. though he had a vague suspicion that the girl had a crush for him, he did not expect her amorous visit at midnight.

', debyoni, why didn't you go to bed? It's past midnight, isn't it?'

'chill winter air is biting me hard. What about you, sotyam? Can't we crush between us and drive away the cold air?'

'no, do please go to your bed. Your dad may be back any moment, 'he said. 'My dad won't be back until Monday morning. He called me from birgaon this afternoon when i was at the school hostel and told me so,' she said, taking his hand and pressing it on her little bosom.

'it is not right,' he said, withdrawing his hand frrom her bosom and gently pushing her from his bed.' what is not right? I am not a virgin any more, you know. I had sex with my cousin subroto once on this very bed and with my classmate roshan I don't exactly remember how many times, in his house when his parents were out of town.'

He was astonished at the cool and calculating way the fifteen year old brat was recounting its sexual affairs.

'that is not the point, debyoni,' satyamied tried to argue.

'don't you have no fear. I always keep a couple of condoms for unexpected opportunities, you know,' she said 'That is not what I mean. You are like my sister,' said satyam.' What nonsense!! a Bengali girl and a mdrasi boy are brother and sister, my foot!' 'no, not that way. You are my guru's daughter. Guru is like a father, isn't he? Please go to your room, please do. Besides, I am not in a mood for it,' he said.

'you—' as a sudden realization dawned on her. 'Now I understand. I had a glimpse of you and bijoy in a close and compromising posture one evening. You are attracted to boys rather than to girls, aren't you. I sure know you are a gay if not a eunuch,' so saying she angrily ran out of the room. Satyam could never erase the memory of that event from his mind all his life.

Satyam could not stay in Calcutta after the incident. He loved debyoni but he did not seek consummation of that love in a secret affair with her. He bade an emotional goodbye to his guru at the house, which was his home for many years and a passionate farewell to bijoy at the houra railway station, left Calcutta and returned to madras to search for a job. He was now eighteen. He had attractive though not smashing good looks. He had a smattering of Hindi and Marathi, besides a working knowledge of writing and speaking bengali. As he had spent his childhood in a village which bordered both the present Karnataka and tiruvallur district in the present tamilnadu, he had a near native fluency in kannada and tamil, besides an excellent oratorical ability in telugu, his mother tongue.

one day while he was hunting for a job in the roads and by-lanes of the city, he met a young man and instantly recognized him as laxman, his school fellow from his native village.

Satyam went up to him and said, 'laxman, don't you recognize me?' 'no chance, oh! Are you satyam?'

'the same. Let us go to some place and talk.' My room is close by. I have been living in Chennai for quite some time now. Let's us go to my room' said laxman.'

'First we will go to a restaurant and eat some food' satyam proposed.' 'no, we will go to my room. I will cook something for both of us.'

On their way to laxman's room, satyam asked his friend, 'how are my people at home. My mother, how is she?'

'Your mother is o. k. but your father is no more. He died of throat cancer. Your mother and Cauvery work as housemaids.'?

What about ganga? she was a cute little angel.' 'her beauty was her undoing. There were several rumors which did the rounds in the village some time ago.'

'Do tell me what happened to her,' shouted satyam, unable to bear the suspense.

'they used to say your mother had an illicit relationship with her maternal uncle, who frequented your house, particularly, after the death of your father. One day on such a visit he found ganga alone in the house and raped her. I am sorry to tell you these harrowing things. She became pregnant and gave birth to a child which was abandoned at the door step of an orphanage. After that she was not seen in the village. They say your brother sold her to a brothel house in Mumbai, what is that place?. red light area. I am sorry to tell you all this'

My sister is my mother. my mother, my grandmother,' satyam murmured. 'what?' laxman asked.' 'Nothing,' he said as did not want to say anything about his debauched biological father.'

'Your brother is well off though. He is a partner in a realtor company in chittor. He is a crook, I am sorry to say. He abandoned your mother and sister to fend for themselves in the village, you see,' laxman said.

satyam, no doubt, had hated his father, who was now no more, but he loved his mother, his brother and his sisters. laxman told him his own tale of woes. having failed to bag even a minor role in a c class film, he fell a victim to the wiles of a small time actor, a middle aged woman, who not only seduced him but turned him into a male sex worker and sent him to the flats of the ageing film actors, the dying flames of the tinsel world till he finally landed in the general hospital near the central station, to be treated for a venereal disease. now he was working as a waiter in a small hotel. having come to madras to act in films, he could not return home and face the derision of his friends, having bragged to them that he would become a film star one day.

satyam had long hair but not a single hair on his cheeks, upper lip and chin. Ram and Krishna, the avatars of god also had smooth cheeks, upper lips and chins in all the paintings as well as in the mythological films they had seen. Gods did not require the services of hair-dressers though the humans considered moustache as a mark of dignity and masculinity. laxman broached his plan to satyam.

'Satyam, I have an idea, I mea n a plan, an enterprise which requires almost no investment. you have some skill as a magician. Why don't you act as a god, I mean a god man. You have long hair. You are not unattractive, in a way,'

Satyam at first laughed at his friend's suggestion. But on reflection he admitted that it was not a bad idea. 'is it right to deceive people?' he asked his friend.

'many men are fleecing the gullible people in the name of religion. One muslim saint in Maharashtra is now worshipped as an avatar of god, isn't he?' 'sai baba, true. but he didn't deceive any one. He didn't make money.

The people made him a god, which was no fault of his. He told people that god was one, whether you called him allah or ram. He was a sincere devotee of god. Gandhi also might be worshipped as god after some time. Aside from this, I am a rationalist. I can't act the role of a god man.'

'which is exactly why you are more fit to don the role of a god man. Like you I am also a rationalist and a communist. We not only earn money, if we succeed, of course, for ourselves but also the poor people of our area. Ends justify means, don't you agree'

then Satyam, though reluctantly, agreed to the plan, in accordance with which, he would reappear in the town near their native village as aanand baba, an avatar of god. He had some savings. He would buy a long enough robe to conceal things which he would produce as miracles. There was magnetism in his large eyes. He knew some slokas from the gita by rote. It would not be difficult for him to mesmerize crowds. Ninety percent of people in the world and ninety nine percent of them in Andhra Pradesh believe in god men. People believe in rebirth. They believe in the other world where there will be celestial sex workers who are always young with fresh and sweet breaths. The people visit every temple, consult every self proclaimed astrologer and worship every man who proclaims himself to be a god man, though they do not throw a little morsel to feed a poor hungry cat.

Satyam and laxman walked to the latter's room in a slum area in kodambakkam. Their plan was to amass wealth and achieve fame. They wanted to take vengeance on the society which treated them badly. satyam could act as a god man without any fear of divine retribution as he did not believe in any divine power and he could take the role of a god man without any qualms because he wanted a job badly, any job and he saw, if their enterprise succeeded, an opportunity to achieve the ultimate objective in his life. He would do anything to alleviate the sufferings of the poor, the destitute and the downtrodden. He knew what demeaning thing poverty was.

Satyam still had a doubt. 'do you think we are going to succeed,' he asked his friend.

'absolutely. People are obsessed with three things, money, sex and god. They approach astrologers to know their future. They blindly believe that the far off planets and stars influence their conduct, character and future. People are so credulous that if someone says that a bull has given birth to a foal, they will ask, without applying their minds, whether it is a colt or a filly. We will make them believe that you are a god man. I have a number of friends in the town to circulate stories about your miracles.'

According to their plan laxman would go to the town near their native village and prepare the way for the entry of a new god man, aanand baba, whose presence exuded piety and divinity. He would produce vibhuti (holy ashes) which would protect people from evil forces and all kinds of diseases. He would bless his followers to prosper in this world and prepare them for a place in swarag. He would instantly produce watches, gold coins, shiv lingas and whatever people wished.

In the meantime satyam would prepare holy ashes from the burnt cowdung mixed with colgate tooth powder, dry ginger, paracetemal tablets and benzoin (sambrani). He would need bags and bags of it. He would also buy some Swiss watches. He had already got a good collection of small shiva lingas made of bronze.

The old chums from school had a happy night dreaming of riches and fame.

Satyam obtained fulfillment after so many days but laxman had a lousy experience as he found himself astride satyam in the middle of the night in a virtual sex act. He realized Satyam was a gay, a homo, who was attracted to boys rather than girls. Satyam, like a sex-starved woman, was kissing all parts of his bare body. Life is, after all, a mixed bag. Good things will come to you only if you bear with somewhat bad things somehow or other.

In india people require permission from the respective authorities to open a shop for doing any business or plying any trade. However, no permission is required to erect makeshift temples on the busy thoroughfares or to set up shops as god men. Satyam as aanand baba and laxman as his devotee and assistant set up their shop, called aanand ashram in a vacant plot near the small town of samimpet. at first business was dull. however, it slowly picked up.

One morning a poor woman came to see baba. Her one year old son had been suffering from fever with high temperature. Aanand baba touched the child and blessed him saying that the child would live for ninety years, two months and seven days. He gave her vibhooti which appeared suddenly as though from nowhere and asked her to mix it in water and feed the child. By the evening the fever subsided and the woman came and fell at his feet. She did not know that baba mixed half a tablet of paracetamol in vibhooti. the woman, as a mark of thanksgiving, donated ten rupees to the ashram. the baba did not touch the money but his assistant grabbed it. the woman had earlier gone to a doctor at first. The lady doctor, who came from a dynasty of medical practitioners, having graduated from a deemed university, paying a hefty amount as capitation fee at the time of admission to the course, had set up her practice recently. She had made the poor child undergo all conceivable tests with no positive result. as the fever did not appear to subside, the poor woman, in desperation, approached the miracle man.

Another day a poor farmer from a village visited baba and lamented that his buffalo was missing. Baba told him that the buffalo was grazing in the coconut grove near the tank of the neighboring village. The buffalo was found there and the farmer gave a small donation which the baba reluctantly accepted.

Sometimes coincidences worked in favor of baba. Sometimes his network of promoters manipulated to make baba's words come true. Baba's popularity as a god man spread to all parts of his native district, chittore, then to other districts and then to the length and breadth of the entire country. Sometimes placebo, sometimes coincidences and sometimes his own network of men and women helped him to fulfill the promises he made to his devotees.

Baba produced watches, shiv lingas and fountain pens and presented them to his distinguished devotees. He learnt from his master, the bengali magician, that If you were able to move your hand faster than the time the brain took to process and register a single image, you could deceive the eyes of the spectators. That is the reason why a series of still pictures moving faster than the brain processes and registers each image, produces the illusion that an object is in movement. There are many other optical illusions which are exploited by magicians and god men alike. A a magician frankly admits that he has performed a trick by a sleight of hand whereas a god man shows it as a miracle achieved through a superhuman power.

Sometimes you feel you have already seen a person, although you see him for the first time.

Ramyani veekshya maduramscha nisamya sabdaan
paryutsuko bhavati yatsukhitopi jantuh
thachetasa smarati noonamabodhapoorvam
bhavasthirani jananaathara souhridani.

the bard believes that when you feel you have already seen or heard a beautiful thing or a sweet sound previously though you see it or hear it for the first time in your life, you are recollecting those things you saw in your previous birth. This is another optical illusion. This is, in actual fact, a fault of the human brain which transfers a particular image from the conscious to the subconscious and then immediately brings it back to register it as though from a past recollection. People believe a Ramakrishna or a Vivekananda saw god. Any tom, dick or harry can see anything in his mind's eye, provided he contemplates it with total concentration for some length of time.

Aanand baba came to be worshipped as an avatar of god. Day in day out, many harebrained foreign devotees, Indian politicians, who had failed to make it to the corridors of power and moviemakers whose films had turned damp squibs at the box office, made a beeline to the baba's extensive ashram, acquired through donations from his devotees. There are people who seek short cuts to earn merit and appease their preferred deities in expectation of wealth in this world and everlasting happiness in the other. baba's empire, built on the mindset of the credulous and superstitious masses, expanded to all major cities in india and abroad. When people succeeded in their efforts, they came to his ashram, thanked baba and made handsome donations to the ashram. When they met with failures in their efforts, they blamed them on their fate and donated bundles of currency notes in the hundi of the ashram all the same.

Though the baba publicly disclaimed and disowned his mother and sisters, declaring that all women in the world were his mothers and sisters, he secretly helped them acquire property beyond their means.

he came to know that his youngest sibling, the quaint little beauty of his family, ganga, having been a victim of a rape, landed in a brothel company in the red light area of Bombay. He dispatched his brother, arjun to Bombay to purchase her release from the company. His brother, who had earlier sold the girl to the brothel house for a handsome amount, now made a hefty profit from the present transaction also. The baba got cauveri married into a respectable family of his relatives. As ganga showed reluctance to get into a matrimonial mode after all her bitter experiences, he made her the head of an orphanage he had founded.

Though he knew that his brother had a reputation as a totally dishonest person, he made him one of the members of the trust he had founded to administer the growing wealth of the ashram. His partner, laxman, was likewise made a trustee.

Some rationalists dared to challenge aanand baba to produce those so called miracles in their presence.

he was a master magician and a fraud, they proclaimed. The watches he produced bore the name and hologram of the Swiss companies that had made them. Baba did not respond to their challenge or criticism. He faced the derision and ridicule of his detractors with calm dignity, saying his mission was not to convert non-believers to believers but to strengthen the belief of the believers. There were many things in the world whose existence could not be tested or proved but they were not any the less real for that.

The baba did not also respond to the mocking letter of debyoni, who, one day, had looked at him with anger, mockery, derision and pity in her big round eyes, when he restrained himself from succumbing to her girlish charms. she wrote to him to call him a pretender and a cheat. he shared her grief for the death of her father, his guru. he was happy that his friend, bijoy had settled in amerce, as a professor in a prestigious university. Her letter showed her pride in her own intellect and the superiority and infallibility of Bengali culture. She believed in the snobbish presumption of every Bengali that Bengal led india in every field of cultural activity. She believed in the hype' 'bengal thinks today what the rest of india will think tomorrow.' She did not give him any credit for his success as a god man either. Rama Krishna, Vivekanandaand and aurobindo much before Andhra god men earned name and fame as great god men. though they misled people, in her opinion, they never resorted to cheating them as he did. Of course, she would never uncover his real persona to the people, knowing fully well that the credulous masses would never believe her words.

child is the mother of woman. The thirty odd year old woman was the same, self confident, self glorifying, self approving, self justifying and self asserting girl he had known her to be. She was right in a way. Bengalis were first in many things. rabindranath Tagore's father was honoured with the title of mahrshi and yet he fathered fourteen Children, the fourteenth being our nobel laureate. Of course, if he had not done so, we would have gone without a national anthem of such artistry and grandeur that common man cannot understand it, which judiciously praises, through polysemy, the earthly emperor, the boss in an office, the don of a mafia gang and the heavenly sovereign, for ruling the minds of people. The poem mentions sind as a region in the indian union, as it was written much before the partition. Pakistan has not protested yet against the inclusion of one of its provinces in the national anthem of india. They may be happy that there is no mention of jammu and Kashmir in the poem. One wonders why the nizam nabob was not honored with the title of devarshi for he was known to have fathered a hundred and twenty children and that too without subjecting a single docile unfortunate woman to undergo labor pains too frequently, for he was known to have one thousand eight hundred concubines besides his eight lawfully wedded wives.

All the people in the world have the tendency to glorify their language, their culture and their country, though they consider self praise an unredeemable weakness of an individual. Bengalis are proud of their language, bengali, which is but mispronounced sanskrit, a sophiticated version of prakrit, a language not spoken by gods but a speech which the marauding indo—european tribes brought from the central asia to the sub-continent with them, who descended not from the head or mind of a deity but from a variety of chimpanzee which started using its brain rather than brawn as it strayed into central asia from its african homeland.

Telugu people quote a former ruler of Andhra who, knowing few languages aside from telugu, said that telugu was the best language in the country for what reason he himsef did not know. Telugu is like an undernourished child with an abnormally bloated belly. It has too many words to refer to the same object or idea and too many objects or ideas are sigmified by the same word. The tamilians assert that tamil is the most ancient language in the world as though every ancient thing is good and adorable. One of their poets has said there is the consonant sound in tamil, zha, which gives nonpareil beauty to tamil. He does not know tamil does not have the full complement and not even the adequate complement of consonant sounds and letters. English people are not far behind in self praise, though they have no originality except in humility and civilized behavior at home and aggressive and domineering conduct abroad. They borrowed their literature from france, their first celebrated poet being a French man, they borrowed their philosophy from the germans and their jurisprudence from the ancient romans and their rhetoric from the ancient greeks. for that matter what is the originality of mankind except a babble of meaningless noises which do but barely and poorly reflect reality? man or even woman cannot produce food from the sun light. Can man produce electricity like the the electric eel? can he recognize the street on which he lives and his own home in his own street without the help of a land mark, whereas a little swallow wings its way thousands of miles to reach its home without a compass? Life is imperfect, inefficient and ephemeral. What chance has man got except to choose the bad from the worse which may again later prove to be better than the bad.

The baba used to climb up a hillock in his ashram every morning and held long spells of dialogue with himself. He used to spend hours at a stretch in contemplation and meditation. He joined his devotees in daily prayers, singing devotional songs loudly. When the journalists asked the baba why he was talking to himself and why he was meditating, being himself a god, baba was silent for some moments. Justice madhavan, a retired judge, now the chairman of the trust, who was present at the time, told the journalists that god was not a being but a becoming. Every person or thing in the universe was a becoming. The baba climbed the hillock to receive divine messages. God was the origin of the message, the messenger and the message itself. the universe was a reflection of god and it was known to be in a flux, self-creating and changing. so god was also known to the rishis to be in a perpetual change. God constantly recreated and reinvented himself. Lord shiva, called swayamhoo, also does penance in his leisure time, I mean when he does not dance with his concert. change was the only reality, the retired judge expounded, answering the query of the journalists. Baba nodded his head approving the explanation given by justice madhavan, though he did not understand a single word that madhavan had uttered.

One day baba called laxman to his private room. 'are you happy now that you are the secretary of the trust. you can sign the checks jointly with arjun as the treasurer.'

'i am happy.'

'You are well off now. How is your wife? How are your kids?' 'they are happy, satyam'

'the main reason why I have become a baba, you know very well, is to serve the people. I don't trust my brother. You must rein his greed.'

'by the bye, did you marry the girl who you had fallen in love with? You told me she was a naidu girl and your father is an orthodox Brahmin.'

'Ya, the same girl. The fat dowry she brought home convinced my parents more than my persuasion that sneha would be an ideal life mate for me.'

'as I said I don't trust my brother. He indulges in all sorts of immoral practices, I understand.'

'you all lived in utter poverty, satyam. Arjun wants his children should not suffer from penury like him. Only thing is he is a bit overdoing it. Once you start amassing wealth there is no way to stop it. wealth intoxicates people more than wine, you know."

'Too true. You are my only friend, laxman. I want to spend more time with you but I can't, you know. You have been inviting rationalists also, I understand, along with religious gurus to give lectures in our colleges for the benefit of the students and staff. That is the only thing we can do to promote rationalism. I understand it had been a difficult job for you to convince the other members of the trust. as an excuse, You invoked the theory of competition of values to save religion, I heard. Thank you for your splendid job.'

They were silent for a few minutes

'you do your work and I will do mine. To get back to the brass-tacks, I need the services of a secretary to look after my correspondence and everything, everything, I mean. He will be my personal assistant. he will be with me day and night, sharing my room. You know what I mean. I spotted one young man on the c c camera the other day. i asked him to meet you sometime next week. He is, I think, an ayyangar boy with a sort of dusky complexion. His name is srinivasan. His father is a temple priest in tirupati. You may interview him and fix his salary. Not much. The Persons who are in need of money serve us better because they have to depend on us. Ok, you have to excuse me for the time being, my dear friend. A central minister is waiting to meet me to receive my blessings. We will find more time to talk later.'

Thus srinivasan became his secretary, personal assistant, close confidante and bed fellow all in one. Nothing succeeds like success, they say. The presidents, prime ministers, chief ministers and other Indian and foreign dignitaries made a bee-line to the baba's now sprawling ashram to receive his blessings and donate money to the ashram.

First, Some visitors to the ashram, the baba thought, sincerely believed that he was a god man and worshipped him. second, Some others, who had no firm notions about god or god men, worshipped him because whether he was god or not, they would lose nothing but some expenses if they received his blessings, for, according to them, none could guess 'which anthill was occupied by which poisonous snake' as they say it in telugu. it was not, according to such people, a bad bargain to try to pull a mountain with a single strand of hair. If they succeeded, the valuable contents of the entire mountain would be theirs and if they failed, they would merely lose a strand of hair, they reasoned. Third, some visited the ashram because their visits would enhance the ratings of their image in the public eye, though they did not believe that he was a god man. Fourth, there were yet some others, the baba thought, they coveted to obtain a share in the vast wealth of the ashram. He also suspected that some crooks visited the ashram for money laundering or to keep their ill-gotten wealth with some members of the trust, who operated their nefarious affairs in the safe precincts of the ashram, without his knowledge.

The baba's empire grew enormously, year after year, under the patronage of successive state and central governments, as the donations from the rich as well as the poor filled the coffers of the ashram. Along with the empire, the stature of the baba as a benefactor of the poor and the needy grew by leaps and bounds.

On the day as his devotees celebrated his fiftieth birth day, a strange incident occurred in the ashram. it was widely reported by the press that there was some shooting in the ashram and a couple of Italians, who came to the ashram to satisfy their curiosity about baba's secret life, were shot dead by his bodyguards. There was a rumor that the two foreigners, who were wandering in the mazes of the vast building where the baba lived, accidentally came upon his bedchamber and found through a half open window the baba in a banaras silk saree, lying on the bed with his personal assistant on top of him. The baba had gold bangles on both his hands. He was fully dressed like a woman in an expensive kanjeevarm silk saree. The Italians discovered to their amazement that the baba was a gay. the bodyguards who got alerted by that time about the presence of the foreigners, apprehended them and reported the matter to the security officer. On the instructions of the chairman of the trust, justice madhavan, the Italians were shot dead, their dead bodies were burnt without a trace and their passports along with their personal belongings were destroyed. The trust had to spend a couple of million U S dollars to cover up the entire embarrassing incident.

Baba was now sixty years of age. He was not actually a bad guy. He was moved by the acute poverty of the great majority of people, particularly, in the villages in the country. In the neighboring district, People had to walk bare foot five to six miles every day to get a pot of drinking water. He himself experienced pangs of hunger as a boy. His parents used to steal paddy from the nearby barn to feed their five children.

He used to stretch his hand, eagerly begging for crumbs of sweets at the sweet shop in the town. His native district was one of the most backward districts in the state. He founded schools, colleges and hostels for the benefit of the poor boys and girls, who were given boarding and lodging facilities free. He founded hospitals for the poor. He donated funds for digging bore wells for the poor farmers who previously depended on the vagaries of weather to irrigate their patches of land. He instructed the trust to cater food and other facilities liberally to the innumerable poor visitors who thronged the ashram every day.

As ardhnaari baba's sharp edge for the enjoyment of creature comforts as well as his urge for sex declined with advancing age, he came to realize that large amounts of money and gold ornaments were siphoned off by the members of the trust, particularly, his brother, arjun. the trustees flew first class in planes and travelled in luxury cars using the trust funds. They purchased for themselves and the members of their families palatial bungalows in Chennai, Bangalore and Mumbai with the trust funds. The baba deceived the ignorant masses through his magic and hypnotism. He was now being cheated, deceived and robbed by a band of crooks and manipulators whom he had trusted and and whom he had inducted into the trust. The main objective of his operation as a god man was to alleviate the sufferings of the poor and the downtrodden masses. Now that his schemes to help the poor were subverted and his main objective was defeated, there was no meaning in continuing his fraud as god man. he would apologize to the people for committing a fraud on their credulity.

Tha baba occasionally had bouts of depression but they became more frequent now. Indra, who seduced his mother and brought him into this inhospitable world, who raped his sister and drove her into prostitution, died in prison, having been convicted guilty of raping a seven year old school girl. He felt that the man surely deserved the punishment. As a great tamil lyricist in one of his finest songs said, a man's feet should not be guided by his eyes and even if his feet were guided by his eyes, his mind should not be led by his feet.

neither the death of his mother, who died, after having been in coma for almost one month nor the death of his sister kaveri, who committed suicide, after having been divorced for not bearing a child, did not affect him much. But the death of ganga saddened his heart. She died of jaundice, having been diagnosed positive for HIV. He could never forget the lovely fac e of his little sister crying her heart out as their father drove him away from home years ago. He failed as a son, as a brother, besides failing as a citizen of the society for donning the garb of a god man to deceive the credulous people through magic and subterfuges. His poverty and his failure to obtain a decent job, lacking proper education and his friend laxman's persuasion had pushed him into this business of a god man. He felt ashamed of his entire life. He lost faith in the people around him. In fact, he lost faith in himself. He was a survivor like his brother, arjun, who was dishonest and corrupt. But was he, in any way, better than arjun?

'Why beholdest thou the mote that is in thy brother's eye, but considerest not the beam that is in thine own eye?'

As he was a rationalist, he always dreaded death. Life seemed to him a journey from nothingness to nothingness. What is the purpose of living, making money or creating values, when death not only the death of an individual but the death of the entire race, collapsing under the weight of its own civilization, or getting destroyed in a cosmic event as an unexpected, unseen and undreamed of black hole, gobbling the sun with its entire entourage, is certain? What is justice? What matters if a person reins his greed and all other passions or willingly submits himself to those passions? Sometimes he spent sleepless nights, counting hours and minutes, waiting for the approaching dawn. During the day time, he is his usual self, insructing and blessing people who visited his ashram. nIght was the time for black thoughts and nightmarish reflections on the futility of human endeavor and existence and finally facing the impending inevitable death.

More than death, he dreaded old age when either the vital organs fail to function, or tend to malfunction. Old age is a living death, the vital organs of the body working at cross purposes, like in a legislative body where everyone tries to produce a noise which no one is able to to hear. What is good for the kidney is not good for the somach and what is nourishing for the liver proves to be harmful to the heart.an old person lives in a virtual purgatory. *vridhatvam jarasa vina* is absolutely impossible. old age without the concomitant of pain and suffering is a figment of imagination. In extreme old age one feels tempted to put an end to one's life, which is worse than death. the organism dies, reaching the end of a genetic program, confirming the illegality of life. It is kleptonomics more than economics, ergonomics or electronics which is at the root of life and death. The amoeba came out of the primeval broth triumphantly, at first, stealing energy, cheating the laws of thermodynamics and finally succumbing to the same laws. Life is stealing something that does not properly belong to it. All are thieves, some people are convicted for theft, some are discharged for want of evidence and others cleverly escape without being caught. Virtue, morality and justice are meaningless in the whirligig of life.

But the balance of convenience appears to be in favor of an orderly life of peaceful compromise with forces not in our cotrol, learning from the experience of past generations, upholding moral and spiritual values and not in favour of a self-destructive and chaotic existence.

As the baba believed he had confidence in the loyalty of his personal assistant, one day, he confided to him and told him that he would dissolve the trust and get a fresh will and testament drawn to revert the entire property to himself. He would not hesitate to admit before the people that he was not a god man but a fraudster and a manipulator, if that was the only course left to stop the fraudulent activities of the pack of swindlers who were misappropriating the funds of the trust. He was ready to face the anger and the derision of the people for committing the gigantic fraud by exploiting their innocence and credulity like other god men in the country. He intended to apologize to the people publickly. enough was enough.' Sufficient unto the day is the evil thereof.' He instructed his personal assistant to call the advocate immediately.

His personal assistant, srinivasan, was not as honest and straight forward as the baba thought of him. he had already swindled out a large amount of money from the trust funds and secretly deposited it in foreign banks. He was not happy with the advances of the old man with a wrinkled face and sagging skin on his cheeks and chin. Instead of calling the advocate as he was instructed by the baba, he disclosed to the chief doctor of the hospital, Dr.mehta, a member of the charitable trust, the intentions of the baba to revoke his will in accordance with the terms of which he had constituted the present trust.

The trustees of the aanand baba ashram held a secret meeting in a five star hotel in Bangalore where they had held such important meetings before and prepared an elaborate secret plan to silence the baba, who was indulging in spending the entire income of the ashram for charitable purposes.

According to their plan, srinivasan would put heroine or viagra in the milk which the baba took after his last meal every night and invite him for sex and work on him so vigorously as to make him lose his breath or stifle him with a pillow and do him in. Once the baba died, they would make a public announcement that the baba was critically ill and he was moved to the hospital's intensive care unit, where nobody would be allowed except the chief doctor and the baba's personal assistant. After three days, they would announce the sad demise of the baba on account of the dysfunctioning of his vital organs. They would put the waxwork figure of the baba in the glass freezer and move it to the prayer hall for facilitating the devotees to pay their last respects to the god man. The freezer would be buried under the bed chamber where his embalmed dead body had already been stowed. after three days they would stage a mock heist, steal the dead body along with the waxwork figure and leave the freezer empty. They would arrange for the destruction of the wax figure along with the dead body of the baba.

They would also employ some crooks to circulate the stories that the baba appeared to them in the flesh, the vibhooti was continuously dropping from the photos of the baba in the houses of his chosen devotees and his footprints were seen in the baba's mandirs built all across the country.

The baba's charitable trust executed its plan to a nicety, using its clout with the police force and the political circles. Thus came to a tragic end the life and activities of one more god man in the country of god men.

last word

the last word is that there can be no last word on absolutely anything in any sphere of human activity, thought and speculation. what is the necessity, at present, for the program enunciated in the foregoing chapters of the book? or is the book a mere symbol? one might ask. for the following among the grounds and reasons, it is both.

why do people the world over learn english as a second language? why do children the world over, with the ambition of becoming tennis stars, start learning to speak english before they start handling racquets? it is not because it has the largest lexicon. it is estimated that there are about a million lexemes or words in english, only a small fraction of which constitutes the common core or the working vocabulary. we don't have to learn english because it an ancient language or because it is easy to learn. modern english is hardly five hundred years old. tamil, one of the most ancient languages in the world, is easier to learn, by far, than english. chinese syntax is more simple than that of english. Hindi(called urdu on theother side of kargil) has more felicity and spontaneity than most other languages to lend itself to lyrical beauty and melody. telugu is more ingenious and resourceful, capable of brilliant innovative techniques than english. Ambiguity, a pejorative term in English, is slesha in telugu, a figure of speech which 'adds to the complexity and richness of poetic language.' there is a unique poetic composition in telugu which narrates both the stories of ramayana and mahabharata simultaneously through the skilful manipulation of sandhi, synonymy, heteronomy and polysemy. french has developed an unparalleled sophistication in evolving a stock of words to accurately name different styles in fashions, cuisine, and different genres in art and literature, as the extensive borrowings of such words from that language into english show. english has borrowed words and expressions from german, a language known to have a rich vocabulary to clearly express every psychological and philosophical concept. every language has a character, an identity and an excellence all its own.

languages for long have separated and divided people. the events of history for the last four hundred years have placed english in the forefront of all other languages to bring the peoples of the world close once again. the world needed one common language to conduct its worldly affairs in the world enormously shrunk by fast transport and electronic communication devices.

the world grabbed the opportunity and accepted english, not through any force but out of sheer necessity, as a common language for the entire world, in spite of strong sentiments and prejudices that normally rule the minds of people, particularly, in the matters of language and culture.

in the process of english emerging as the lingua franca of the world the native speakers of english have lost as much as they have gained. english no longer exclusively belongs to any particular nation or community. it now truly belongs to the world. everyone gains and no one loses, if we make english more simple without affecting, in any way, its identity, character and resourcefulness.

all natural languages are replete with redundancies, superfluous conventions and complex and convoluted devices, reflecting the primitive human beings' belabored struggle to communicate in the dim origins of human civilization. those conventions were once probably good and useful too but they are at present dead wood, to be disposed of as such. as alexander fleming said, "a good thing, if it is a really good thing, disappears giving way to a better thing".

hence there is now a compelling necessity for deliberate and well-conducted interventions to turn living languages into more simple, user-friendly and efficient tools of communication. there is all the more reason for english, being a global language, with a vast expanding vocabulary, to be made more simple and more free from unmeaning conventions.

though the human brain functions marvelously to receive, store, organize, retrieve and reproduce information, its capacity is not unlimited. it is already so heavily burdened with myths and legends created by the imaginative minds of the past and the present that it may be rendered, not in the distant future, incapable of making a clear distinction between reality and illusion, the present and the past. there are some programs which are fanatically adhered to, though they have outlived their use and have been proved to be totally unproductive, besides being divisive and dangerous. the adage "less luggage more comfort" equally applies to the long and precarious journey of the human brain, grappling with enormously ever increasing large volumes of information.

english has an inbuilt mechanism to absorb words and expressions from other languages with a remarkable facility. but indiscriminate borrowing may prove a bane rather a benefit. several languages have suffered from this tendency so much so that they are burdened with large vocabularies for no real advantage though. what good is it if you have a dozen words for a monkey but no word for a lowly garden plant like spinach?

In telugu 'hari' means 1.vishnu, 2.indra, 3.sun, 4.moon, 5. yama, 6. Lion, 7.horse, 8.monkey, 9.snake, 10.air, 11.ray, 12.frog and 13.parakeet as a noun and if it is used as an adjective it means 1. green and 2. olden. this is because the telugu pundits of the past indulged in excessive and indiscriminate borrowing of words from Sanskrit to show off their scholarship, thus doing irreparable damage to the language as a vehicle of clear, unambiguous, accurate and effective communication system. english has never suffered from the surfeit of words as the additional words are put to new uses or allowed to die, having failed to compete with their rivals or for want of patronage from discerning users. To give an example, oxford thesaurus gives the following words as synonyms: 1. ravishing, 2.gorgeous, 3.stunning, 4. Alluring, 5.lovely, 6.attractive, 7.pretty, 8.handsome, good-looking, 9.pleasing, 10. comely, 11. charming, 12. delightful, 13. glamorous, 14.graceful, 15.elegant and 16.beautiful. however, such is the genius of the language that not even an inept or inexperienced practitioner of english will be tempted to use elegant in the place of beautiful or lovely instead of attractive or gorgeous for stunning.

there is, in english, an inherent capacity to internally create new words and expressions through class conversion, which is one of the most productive features of the language.

"any part of speech can be used as any other part of speech" sounds like a publicity hype but it is true to a considerable extent. english words are more secular than the words of any language not because it has now become an international language of science, technology and business communication but because no creed or religion has ever taken a strong root in england, its people always standing by secular institutions in preference to religious ones. the people of england have never been swayed by bitter religious or racial controversies and conflicts that have often raged in the rest of europe and the world.

in spite of all its inherent merits, qualifying it as one fit to be an international language and in spite of its simple and to some extent logical syntax, english, in its present form, is not easy to learn. the number of people who use it as their second language across the world outnumber its native speakers at least by two to one. there is an urgent need to liberate english from unmeaning conventions, obscure idiom, obsolete structures and irrational spelling for making it more simple and less problematic without, in any way, affecting its character and effectiveness.

learn and <u>teach</u> english easiest, fastest, and surest through reverse process. discover acceptable and avoid not so acceptable structures through reasoning.

the book, <u>toward a more simple, plain and rational English,</u> all about these and much more. capitalization, the device used only in writing with no corresponding device in speech, does not give any tangible advantage to the users of the language. most other languages have no similar capitalization and they have lost nothing in clarity either. on the other hand, capitalization makes an altogether unnecessary heavy demand on the keyboard. the traditions, which have lost their usefulness and relevance, need not be adhered to in the matter of language as well as life in general. good things, if they are really good things, give way to better things. spelling needs to be changed in order to reflect speech. at present there are two different varieties of the language, the spoken and the written. dictionaries and children's workbooks should suggestalternative more rationalized spellings.

The so called unacceptable structures, if they make the language more simple, should be adopted. <u>seed</u> and <u>goed</u> often heard in children's' speech should be adopted as alternative forms of <u>saw</u> and <u>went</u> as <u>waked</u> and <u>awaked</u> are no longer unacceptable alternatives, at least in some major varieties of the language.

Grammar, an effective tool to teach and learn english, has needlessly been elevated to the status of an enigmatic science, inaccessible to the users of the language, by chomsky and his enthusiastic followers who have been fruitlessly indulging in the exercise of inventing newer words and techniques to analyze the language, thus complicating the process of learning instead of simplifying it. we know that there is no need to form a sentence through a mathematical formula, for language learning is easier and more accessible to the human brain than mathematics. We learn mathematics through language and not the other way about.

Languages should not be allowed to entirely determine the thought processes and behavioral patterns of the people and people should determine the structure of a language. Languages, invented by primitive people though, progressively changed and got adapted to the needs of present day man. it should be strengthened further through well directed interventions.